# TEACHING & TESTING
# INFORMATION LITERACY SKILLS

Jane Bandy Smith, Ph.D.

Lisa Churchill and Lucy Mason
Contributors

Linworth
Books

Professional Development Resources for K-12
Library Media and Technology Specialists

To the children who make life so grand:

Ella, Will, Catherine, Stuart, Elizabeth, Foster, Roman, and Julian

Library of Congress Cataloging-in-Publication Data

Smith, Jane Bandy.
    Teaching & testing information literacy skills / Jane Bandy Smith ; Lisa
Churchill and Lucy Mason.
        p. cm.
    Includes bibliographical references and index.
    ISBN 1-58683-078-3 (pbk.)
    1. Information literacy—Study and teaching (Elementary)—United States. 2.
Information literacy—Skills and teaching (Secondary)—United States. 3.
Information retrieval—Study and teaching (Elementary)—United States. 4.
Information retrieval—Study and teaching (Secondary)—United States. I. Title:
Teaching and testing information literacy skills. II. Churchill, Lisa. III. Mason,
Lucy. IV. Title.
ZA3075.S57 2005
028.7—dc22
                                    2004026004


Author: Jane Bandy Smith, Ph.D.

Linworth Books:
Carol Simpson, Editorial Director
Judi Repman, Associate Editor

Published by Linworth Publishing, Inc.
480 East Wilson Bridge Road, Suite L
Worthington, Ohio 43085

ISBN: 1-58683-078-3

5 4 3 2 1

# Table of Contents

# List of Figures and Tables

# Foreword

An old and often-quoted adage concerns the difference between giving a man a fish to sustain him for a day or teaching him how to fish, which can sustain him through life. Likewise, many books offer activity-filled lessons for school librarians to use in teaching students information literacy skills. Those activity books are useful, but they provide a media specialist with a fish instead of teaching the skill of fishing. This book shows a library media specialist how to teach and test information literacy skills in ways that will nourish the school program.

# Preface

> A popular government without popular information or the means of acquiring it is but a prologue to a farce or a tragedy, or perhaps both.
>
> *- James Madison, principal framer of the First Amendment*

Change is slow but steady in school libraries. Years ago students went to the school library to check out books. Later it was the site of a weekly class where students learned library skills. Today the media center is fast becoming a literacy laboratory where students access and use information in ways that enrich classroom experiences. Applying information skills to coursework helps them become proficient. The transition is underway but far from finished. The change will not be complete until every student is engaged routinely in using information resources as a means of learning course content. The school library's reach goes beyond its walls; its resources are available in many places—in the media center, online in the classroom, and online from other institutions or agencies. When the transition is complete, media specialists and teachers will be engaged continuously in planning and evaluating, with both professionals assuming responsibility for student success.

Today's library media professionals—whether they are called school librarians, media specialists, teacher librarians, or resource teachers—have a golden opportunity to contribute to school improvement, and information literacy is the pathway. Information literacy is a common concern of both teachers and media specialists. Administrators and parents need to understand how these skills can help students perform better. They need to know that students who understand how information is organized can apply those organizational principles to retrieving and organizing their course information. Students who are skillful in interpreting, summarizing, inferring, and otherwise mentally manipulating information to determine its use and worthiness will be better students and better citizens. Students who have a thirst for knowledge and who know how to find the information they want will prosper in every endeavor. The school community needs to understand the media specialist's role is to help students use information and value knowledge instead of just helping them locate resources.

Change is underway, but it requires pressure from peers and leaders. As Michael Fullan reminds us, change is complex, loaded with uncertainty, requires both top-down and bottom-up initiatives, and begins within each individual (19-41). Change is challenging but the time is right because the nation is looking for answers that will result in better schools. Information literacy is one answer but the community may overlook it unless media specialists push the change.

Fullan, Michael. *Change Forces: Probing the Depths of Educational Reform.* London: Falmer, 1993.

# Acknowledgments

Many individuals encouraged and supported this book's development and the author is grateful for their enthusiasm and interest. Special appreciation goes to Lisa Churchill and Lucy Mason, two of the best people I know working in schools. It is thrilling to have their reports included in the book. I am grateful to Mr. Keith Berry, Science Teacher at Gresham Middle School and to Miss Rachael LaMonte, Language Arts Teacher at Berry Middle School for their willingness to share their professional experiences. My appreciation is also extended to the school administrators in Jefferson County and Hoover City, specifically Dr. Jack Farr, Superintendent of the Hoover City Schools; Dr. Kathleen Wheaton, Principal of Berry Middle School; Dr. Phil Hammonds, Superintendent of the Jefferson County Schools; Mrs. Gloria Dennard, Director of Library Media/Instructional Supplies for the Jefferson County Schools, and Mr. Rodney B. Johnson, Principal of Gresham Middle School.

I am grateful to the many Alabama educators who provided resources and suggestions included in this book: Margaret Blake, Director of Technology for the Mobile County Schools, and to the following Mobile County Schools personnel: Violet Lowery, Supervisor of Library Media Services; Terri Baker, O'Rourke Elementary School; Janet Carlson, Shepard Elementary School; Barbara Carlton, Hall Elementary School; Kay Johnson, Meadowlake Elementary School; Denise Lyda, Semmes Elementary School; Melanie Adkins, Clark School of Math and Science; Betty Hall, Chastang Middle School; Janell Kyranakis, Baker Middle School; Elaine Richards, Semmes Middle School; Mary Anne Bemis, Bryant High School; Gloria Bush, Davidson High School; Jeanetta Hunter, Rain High School; Kathryn Smith, Satsuma High School; Phyllis Truly, Montgomery High School; and Dr. Carolyn Lee Taylor, Assistant Superintendent of Curriculum and Instruction, who granted permission to use the Mobile material.

Appreciation goes to Jenny B. Salladay, Library Information Specialist, Lebovitz Resource Center, McCallie Middle School in Chattanooga for letting me include examples of two interesting collaborative projects at her school. Thanks, too, to Jeff Kurtzman who helped originate the Presidential Primaries Project and to Dr. Jerome J. Ferrari for directing the Holocaust Project.

A tip-of-the-hat to Dr. Kent Gustafson of the University of Georgia, who permitted me to adapt his instructional development checklist for this book. Thanks to Donna Fuller, Technology Specialist at the Alabama State Department of Education, who provided technical expertise in developing the manuscript.

Many thanks to the professionals at Linworth Publishing, especially Marlene Woo-Lun, Publisher and President of Linworth Publishing, Donna Miller, Donna King, and Betty Morris. Finally, I want to thank my husband, Bill David Smith, for his support.

# INTRODUCTION

There is not a standardized curriculum or standardized test for information skills, although items included on various tests measure some of these skills. However, the library media profession is moving in the right direction by defining information literacy and establishing learning goals for students in kindergarten through college. If our profession continues to act in a thoughtful manner, the growing importance of information literacy can evolve as greater support for library media services. For this to happen, school librarians will need to be both information and teaching specialists who can explain how information literacy skills help individuals succeed in school, work, and life. They must also know how to work with teachers to plan, deliver, and test instruction effectively.

## The Book's Purpose

This book helps a library media specialist translate the philosophical statements and student information literacy standards found in *Information Power: Building Partnerships for Learning* into action. Those actions will improve student performance because information literate students will be able to access, use, and evaluate information in a more proficient and efficient manner. Students who know how information is organized and who have internalized a questioning approach to information will be better able to utilize information.

Student performance must improve before education is more highly regarded and valued by the public. Because of frequent reports about poor test performance of U.S. students, the public in general and governing bodies in particular are unhappy with the current situation. Today schools are under enormous pressure to improve student performance. When teachers and administrators see how information literacy skills can help students learn more subject matter and improve test performance, they will join forces with the library media specialists. For this to happen, the media specialist must be able to explain what information literacy skills are and to show how knowing these skills can improve student performance.

Information in this book will help a school librarian who can manage a school library, but has no experience as a teacher. The book presents a process to use in translating the student learning standards into teachable units integrated with the school curriculum. This process is explained and illustrated with two media specialists sharing their experience using the process described in this book.

Current professional literature for the school media specialist contains little information about effective evaluation. Although this situation is beginning to change, change is slow. The fact that testing is addressed in this book makes it stand out among the titles currently in print. In summary, there are three reasons to purchase this book: it validates the relevance of library media programs to school improvement; provides a useable curriculum for information literacy instruction; and extends and enhances professional knowledge about teaching and testing.

## Style of Writing

The book is written in clear, concise, and active language. Numerous tables and checklists summarize the information presented in the text and make it easier for readers to grasp the procedures.

## The Book's Contents

The first chapter is an overview of events and publications that have resulted in information literacy being accepted today as important skills. Chapter two investigates how instructional models, such as critical thinking and study systems, have transformed traditional library skills into information literacy skills. Chapter three uses a traditional approach to curriculum development to offer an information literacy curriculum for grades kindergarten through 12 founded on the first three student learning standards presented in *Information Literacy: Building Partnerships for Learning*. Chapter four borrows curriculum from science teachers. "Habits of mind" refers to the mindset of a scientist at work. This author believes students need to develop a similar mindset when handling information.

Chapter five provides advice about curriculum implementation, supporting collaboration with teachers as the best implementation method and suggesting several things for a library media specialist to do in order to be ready to collaborate. Chapter six is an overview of what we know about effective teaching. It examines teaching philosophies and methods, and then offers eight ways to improve teaching. Chapter seven explains what the literature has to say about effective testing. It explains the three types of tests used most often in schools, presents a variety of testing techniques, and suggests some points to consider when developing a test. Chapter eight moves step-by-step from curriculum to lesson planning, and provides a number of examples that illustrate the final product. Two middle-school library media specialists, who are known for their student-centered programs, contributed chapter nine to the book. Each one put the procedures presented in this book into action and they share their experiences. It could be said that chapter nine is proof of the pudding! These are real-life situations where the media specialists and classroom teachers planned, taught, and tested units in which the course content drove information skill development.

An introductory quote begins each chapter to share a similar point of view or to challenge the reader's thinking. Numerous tables and figures condense information in an effort to promote comprehension. Four checklists provide easy rules-of-thumb to judge collaborating, teaching, testing, and instructional planning.

# About the Author

Jane Bandy Smith's career has taken her into school libraries, classrooms, administrative offices, and state agencies. She recently retired from the Alabama Department of Education where she served as a technology specialist, the school library media consultant, and coordinator of instructional assistance. Dr. Smith moved to the Alabama agency from the Georgia Department of Education where she coordinated field services for the Division of Instructional Media. Before beginning work in state agencies, she taught library media and education courses at the University of Georgia, West Georgia College, and the University of Alabama in Birmingham. Although she spent time as director of the Education Library at the Tuscaloosa campus of The University of Alabama, her career began as an elementary school librarian in a school less than a mile away.

Dr. Smith has presented hundreds of professional development programs for school systems and professional organizations. Her books include *Achieving a Curriculum-Based Library Media Center Program*, *Research for School Media Specialists* (with Kent Gustafson), *Renewal at the Schoolhouse* (with Ben Carson), and *Library Media Center Programs for Middle Schools*. She contributed to *Helping Kids Learn Multicultural Concepts* and edited the *School Library Media Annual* (Vols. 6-10). For more than 30 years, Dr. Smith's work has focused on how the library media center contributes to a school's instructional program.

# 1

# The Growing Importance of Information Literacy

> ...there also exists the potential of addressing many long-standing social and economic inequities. To reap such benefits, people—as individuals and as a nation—must be information literate.
>
> *"Information Literacy: Final Report, January, 1989."*

On the first page of its final report, the American Library Association's Presidential Committee on Information Literacy proposed information skills as a way to level society's playing field. The benefit this book promises is more limited, but still ambitious. It proposes that an information literate student will perform better in the classroom and on those standardized tests that the public sees as paramount evidence of a school's worth. These claims are made because an information literate student knows:

- How information is organized and uses this knowledge to speed-up content acquisition,
- How to recognize creditable information,
- How to locate additional, pertinent information beyond the text book,
- How to analyze information in order to identify important elements, and
- How to organize information and to present it in the appropriate format.

Information literate students are not distracted or consumed with irrelevant information so they hone in on the most important data. They are skillful in connecting new information with things already known so they can grapple with new situations and solve problems by applying what they know. A student who can locate information can add to the limited material found in textbooks to suit personal interests. A student who previews and raises questions about a chapter or article before reading or viewing it is more primed and responsive to the information being presented.

Cognitive researchers tell us that gifted students innately apply information-handling skills. When presented with new information, they can combine it with existing knowledge and apply it to a new situation in an organized manner. Gifted students can:

- Handle abstractions,
- Draw inferences,
- Relate cause and effect,
- Conceptualize and synthesize,
- Make generalizations, and
- See relationships (Eric 4-5).

These are information literacy skills because they are skills that aid an individual in drawing meaning from informational sources. Each of these skills involves the mental manipulation of information that helps discern meaning. If these skills are innate to gifted students, who use them to perform better in class and on tests, they should be taught to all students to help them perform better. Average students who are information literate may not be able to perform as well as gifted students, but if these skills were taught they would be better equipped to bring the same strengths to various learning situations.

Information literacy is not only important in a school setting; the business community now sees these skills as fundamental to job success. According to a survey conducted by the U.S. Department of Labor, employers believe an ability to locate and handle information is among the most important skills an employee must have (3). An information literate worker is better able to compete in today's competitive, global, and rapidly changing job market. Just as the marketplace has broadened from a local to an international perspective, a competitor's knowledge has had to broaden. Because available information has increased dramatically, there is more to know and no one can retain adequate knowledge; instead, it is necessary to know where and how to find the information one needs. Having the right information at the right time is a key to success. For example, a person who knows about a job opening has a chance of getting it. A manufacturer improves his profit margin if he can locate a cheaper source of raw materials. A worker who solves a company's quality control problem is more likely to be promoted. Success is based in large measure on getting accurate, adequate, and timely information—an information literate person can do this.

The term literacy was used as early as the 1970s, but it was not used routinely by librarians and educators until the 1990s (Cohen par. 1). Now the term is used in many fields and librarians are gaining confidence from others' support. For many years, librarians had stressed the importance of people knowing how to use library systems to find specific information and being able to evaluate and analyze the information they found. Now other educators, business leaders, and government leaders are joining them to support information literacy as skills basic to lifetime success.

Recently, four paths merged to promote the importance of information literacy. One path is the growing outcry for better schools, which has caused educators to look for remedies. A second path is the library community agreeing on a definition for information literacy and establishing skill development standards for grades kindergarten through college. A third and important path is the recognition by content disciplines that information literacy is a set of essential skills embedded in their subject areas. The fourth path is an explosion in the use of personal computers and online databases by the general public. Perhaps the fourth path is the most dynamic because it created a public awareness about the intricacies of locating pertinent and valid information. As these four paths have merged, information literacy has become a recognized and important area of study. Figure 1.1 illustrates these influential paths.

This chapter continues by exploring each path and examining events of the past two decades that have brought information literacy to the forefront.

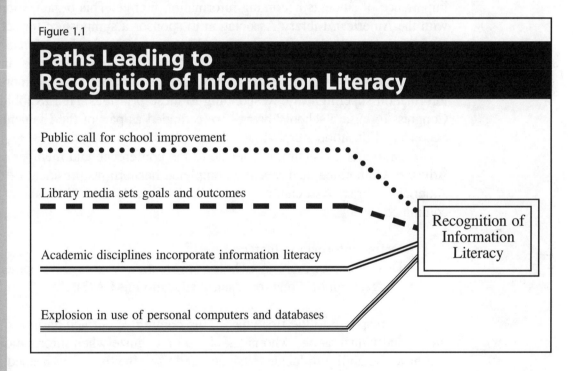

Figure 1.1

**Paths Leading to Recognition of Information Literacy**

Public call for school improvement

Library media sets goals and outcomes

Academic disciplines incorporate information literacy

Explosion in use of personal computers and databases

Recognition of Information Literacy

# The Public Demands Better Schools

In 1983, a scathing report on public school performance began a public cry for improvement. When released by the U.S. National Commission on Excellence in Education, *A Nation at Risk* was a shot across the bow of schools, colleges, universities, and professional education organizations. Vows to improve public schools came from governors' offices to individual classrooms. Educators at every level and in every discipline reacted. Everyone was embarrassed by the revelations of poor school performance in the United States.

Library organizations were also jolted by the report. They began to study how they could help improve our nation's schools. The National Commission on Libraries and Information Science (NCLIS), an agency established by Congress in 1970 to advise the federal government on national library and information policy, contributed to the effort. NCLIS issued a concept paper in 1986 that urged the federal government to support strong school media centers and to emphasize the importance of students becoming information literate. This organization joined with the American Library Association to sponsor a symposium for school media professionals and other educators. NCLIS was an organizational force behind the 1991 White House Conference on Library and Information Services, in which the top priorities were strengthening library services for youth and promoting the information superhighway. Responding to these priorities, NCLIS lobbied Congress to ensure school libraries were funded as part of the Elementary and Secondary Education Act (7-8).

Margaret Chisholm, a delegate to the conference and member of its Advisory Committee, had recently completed her term as president of the American Library Association (ALA). While President of ALA, she named a committee to:

- Define information literacy,
- Design one or more models for information literacy development, and
- Suggest implications for teacher education (ALA 7).

In response to the first charge, the committee defined an information literate individual as one who is "... able to recognize when information is needed and have the ability to locate, evaluate, and use effectively the needed information" (ALA 1). The committee recommended forming a coalition of organizations to promote information literacy and the National Forum on Information Literacy (NFIL) resulted. NFIL is a coalition of more than 70 education-related organizations that promotes information literacy as universally needed skills. The organization has spawned a number of projects in the United States and abroad to promote information literacy. One project encourages teacher education programs to assure that teachers-in-training understand the value of information skills and know how to teach these skills to students (NFIL 2).

Among those serving on the ALA Presidential Committee were prolific authors who wrote about the importance of information literacy as a viable skill set. Patricia Senn Breivik, chair of the committee, co-authored a pamphlet about information literacy for school principals that was published by the National Education Association (1998). Her effort was crucial because it forged a bond of common interest among classroom teachers, school administrators, and school librarians. Committee member Carol Kuhlthau prepared a review of research related to information skills instruction for the ERIC Clearinghouse on Information Resources and edited a compilation of articles about information literacy that were published previously in *School Library Media Quarterly*.

In addition to her publications, she also chaired the Information Skills Task Force for the American Association of School Librarians.

The Association of Supervision and Curriculum Development, one of the NFIL Organizations, issued a statement that information literacy should be part of every student's experience. This endorsement was a major impetus for information literacy to be accepted by educators as a creditable area of study because ASCD is a national organization of education leaders from schools and universities. To support their policy statement, the organization formed the ASCD Information Literacy Network to help encourage implementation of information skill instruction in schools. Readers interested in this network will find a contact number in the sources cited section at the end of this chapter.

## Library Media Standards and Information Literacy

Upon release of *A Nation at Risk*, two major school media associations joined together to clarify how school media services contributed to school performance. In 1988 the American Association of School Librarians and the Association of Educational Communications and Technology issued professional guidelines that emphasized the importance of school media centers supporting school instructional programs (AASL/AECT). The new guidelines stressed the role of the school library media specialist instead of emphasizing how collection quantity improved the school program. A three dimensional role was set forth for a school media specialist that included being:

- an information specialist,
- a teacher, and
- an instructional consultant (AASL/AECT, *Guidelines* 117-23).

As part of being an information specialist, every media professional was expected to develop expertise in using electronic media for communication and information retrieval. Although the school media profession embraced the title of the 1988 publication, *Information Power*, there was general discontent with the "instructional consultant" role because few practitioners understood the responsibilities related to it and teachers generally rejected it. So when new guidelines were published in 1998, the title remained *Information Power*, but the new subtitle emphasizes the importance of librarian and teacher partnerships. The earlier three-part role was replaced by a four-part role that includes:

- teacher,
- information specialist,
- instructional partner instead of consultant, and
- program administrator.

The cornerstone for *Information Power: Building Partnerships for Learning* is found in its first two words of text: "information literacy." Perhaps its most lasting contribution is the section, "Information Literacy Standards for Student Learning" (8-44). After stating the learning standards, the guide shows how the standards relate to each school discipline. As one might expect, release of the information standards has spawned a multitude of papers, books, articles, workshops, and conferences.

At last there seems to be a purposeful program whereby the school media specialist can prove the impact of media services on school performance. Such proof has long been sought. In 1982, Didier found the reading skills of students improved in schools where there was a professionally staffed media center. Lance, Welborn, and Hamilton-Pennell built on Didier's findings when they found a positive correlation between library staff, collection size, and academic achievement through a Colorado school survey (Lance et al., 1993). Replication of that study in Alaska and Pennsylvania and a repeat study in Colorado yielded similar positive correlations (Lance et al., 1999, 2000, 2002). These studies are important because they suggest that media services and collections contribute to academic achievement, but the library media profession needs evidence that shows student performance improves as a direct contribution. Information skill instruction provides that avenue.

A joint task force of representatives from the American Association of School Librarians (AASL) and the Association of College and Research Libraries (ACRL) recommended ways for librarians at all school levels to cooperate. One recommendation called for development of standards for college students. As a result, the Board of Directors of the Association of College and Research Libraries approved a set of five standards and 22 performance indicators for college students in January 2000 (5-13).

# The Effect of Content Standards on Information Literacy

After *A Nation at Risk* was released, educators in every discipline were motivated to analyze and improve curriculum delivery. However, the standard-setting process at the national level requires broad, sustained communication between practitioners and academicians and is an expensive undertaking. Organizations representing content disciplines were at different stages in the process of reconsidering established content standards. When the U.S. Congress passed the Goals 2000 legislation stating school improvement goals, they also passed enabling legislation that provided money so educators in the various disciplines could develop new content standards. Some of these funds were also used to train teachers in more effective techniques. Recently improved math scores for United States students give evidence these funds were used as intended.

Information literacy can now be found in every national curriculum document establishing a connection between information literacy and the content standards. Table 1.1 illustrates how information literacy is incorporated in standards for mathematics, language arts, science, and social studies. This common interest is encouraging teacher-librarian cooperation. Practitioners such as Zorana Ercegovac point out the mutual interests of both teachers and librarians who today teach a "… cut-and-paste generation, ensuring that teenagers become creative thinkers, stressing to students that not all information is credible and when it's appropriate to cite sources" (53).

Table 1.1

# Content Standards and Information Literacy

| Discipline | Title of Standards | Organization | Incorporates Literacy |
|---|---|---|---|
| **Mathematics 1989** | *Curriculum and Evaluation Standards for School Mathematics* | National Council of Teachers of Mathematics | Defines information literacy as including<br>• Problem solving<br>• Estimation<br>• Thinking strategies<br>• Formulating<br>• Investigating<br>• Using computers & other technologies |
| **Social Studies 1994** | *Curriculum Standards for the Social Studies* | National Council for the Social Studies | Uses two headings to categorize Information Literacy, (1) "Skills Related to Acquiring Information" and (2) "Skills Related to Organizing and Using Information." Skills include<br>• Investigate sources<br>• Examine pictures and artifacts<br>• Paraphrase<br>• Use maps & globes<br>• Interpret & infer<br>• Record sources<br>• Reason<br>• Quote sources<br>• Develop timelines<br>• Recognize different perspectives<br>• Use cross references |
| **Science 1995** | *Science for All* | National Committee on Science Education Standards & Assessment | Uses information literacy as a heading for<br>• Inquiry process<br>• Decision-making<br>• Investigation skills<br>• Critical thinking skills<br>• Ability to access, evaluate, and use information |
| **English 1996** | *Standards for the English Language Arts* | National Council of Teachers of English & the International Reading Association | Uses three content standards (#s 7, 8, and 11) to address the following skills<br>• Conduct research<br>• Use a variety of technological and information resources<br>• Participate as members of literacy communities |

# The Information Explosion Impacts Information Literacy

Information literacy is increasingly important because of the explosion in available information and the use of home computers for electronic information retrieval. Greater access has promoted greater awareness about the need for skill development. People who navigate the Internet know the information explosion is real and not just a catchy phrase. Lyman and Varian remind us that "the world produces between 1 and 2 exabytes of unique information per year, or roughly 250 megabytes for every man, woman and child on earth" (1). Searching for specific information has become somewhat like shopping in a large grocery store for a particular type of cereal. There are so many choices that it is hard to find the exact kind you want. Oberman believes the cereal syndrome makes us realize that having many choices often makes life harder, not easier.

Electronic data searching is both exhilarating and frustrating. It is exciting because it places so much information at an individual's fingertips, but it can be frustrating because it is often quite difficult to ferret out specific information, and in some instances reliable information. The more an individual searches the Internet, the more he discovers much of the information is unedited and sometimes biased. These experiences stress how much we need evaluation skills. To ensure students will not drown in the sea of information, we must provide them with a safety net called information literacy skills (Oberman 39).

Table 1.2 provides an overview of the events that have moved information literacy to the forefront.

# The Professional Challenge of Information Literacy

Many media specialists remain uncertain about how to implement an information literacy program in their schools. This situation exists despite the well-stated performance standards and the content applications included in the latest *Information Power*. They accept the document's professional challenge to ensure all students and staff become discriminating consumers and creators of information, but that challenge seems daunting. Media specialists express a need for greater definition and detail. They know a discriminating consumer of information should be able to determine the quality and usefulness of any information they access, but many questions remain.

- How can a discriminating consumer and skilled creator be evaluated?
- At what level is competency or literacy accomplished?
- What is meant by comprehensive instruction?
- How can information literacy instruction be structured across grades?
- How are information skills related to the school curriculum?
- What are the best ways to teach and test these skills?
- How do you demonstrate the impact of skill instruction on performance?

Library media specialists believe information literacy skills will empower students to go beyond the limited information found in textbooks. They know these skills enable students to identify missing information; to locate, access, and

Table 1.2

# Events Promoting Information Literacy

|  | Event | Sponsor | Impact |
|---|---|---|---|
| 1982 | **Publication** *A Nation at Risk* | National Commission of Excellence in Education | Raised public awareness concerning failing schools |
| 1985 | **Invited Meeting** Librarians, administrators | National Commission on Libraries & Information Services (NCLIS) | Sought clarification of the media specialist's role in teaching information skills |
| 1986 | **Publication** "Educating Students to Think" | NCLIS | Presented a conceptual framework for teaching information skills |
| 1987 | **Publication** *Information Skills for an Information Society* | Educational Resources Information Clearinghouse Carol Kuhlthau, ed. | Summarized current knowledge |
| 1988 | **Standards** *Information Power: Guidelines for School Library Media Programs* | Association for Educational Communications & Technology (AECT) American Association of School Librarians (AASL) | Specified information specialist as role for library media specialist |
| 1989 | **Report** | ALA Presidential Committee on Information Literacy | Promoted cooperation and generated organization activities |
| 1990 | **Recommendation** | National Forum on Information Literacy (NFIL) | Encouraged teacher/librarian collaboration in teaching students information literacy |
| 1991 | **Report** "What Work Requires of Schools" | U.S. Department of Labor | Validated information literacy as job success skills |
| 1991 | **Publication** (Special Issue) "Restructuring and School Libraries" *NASSP Bulletin* | National Association for Secondary School Principals | Brought attention of school administrators to information skill instruction |
| 1992 | **Report** | NFIL | Adopted outcomes for an information literate student |
| 1994 | **Legislation** Goals 2000: Educate America Act | U.S. Congress | Established goals to improve American education |
| 1994 | **Position Paper** "Information Literacy" | AASL | Adapted a paper from Wisconsin association for Board adoption |
| 1995 | **Publication** "Information Literacy: Philosophy, Principles and Practice" | *International Association of School Librarians School Libraries Worldwide* | Brought information literacy instruction to an international library audience |
| 1998 | **Publication** *Information Literacy: Educating Children for the 21st Century*, 2nd ed. | Breivik & Senn, National Education Association (NEA) | Promoted involvement of the total school staff in ensuring students become information literate |
| 1998 | **Standards** *Information Power: Building Partnerships for Learning* | AECT & AASL | Established standards for student instruction in information literacy |
| 1998 | **Taskforce** "Blueprint for Collaboration" | Association for College and Research Libraries (ACRL) and AASL | Promoted collaboration between school and college libraries in teaching information literacy |
| 2000 | **Standards** *Information Literacy Competency Standards* | ACRL | Established information literacy standards for college students |

extract it, and then use it to communicate, to solve problems, or to make decisions. They realize the potential, but getting from the promise to the practice is a big step. This book helps media specialists take that step.

## Sources Cited

American Association of School Librarians. Association for Educational Communications and Technology. *Information Power: Building Partnerships for Learning.* Chicago: American Library Association, 1998.

American Association of School Librarians. Association for Educational Communications and Technology. *Information Power: Guidelines for School Library Media Programs.* Chicago: American Library Association, 1988.

American Library Association. Presidential Committee on Information Literacy. "Information Literacy: Final Report, January, 1989" in *Information Literacy: Learning How to Learn.* Carol C. Kuhlthau, Ed. Chicago: American Library Association, 1991.

Association for Supervision and Curriculum Development (ASCD), Information Literacy Network, call 1-800-933-ASCD for information.

Association of College and Research Libraries. American Association of School Librarians. "Blueprint for Collaboration: AASL/ACRL Task Force on the Educational Role of Libraries." <http://www.ala.org/acrl/blueprint.html> or "Information Literacy: Competency Standards for Higher Education," *Teacher Librarian* 28.3 (2001): 9-16.

Breivik, Patricia Senn, and J.A. Senn. "Information Literacy: Educating Children for the 21st Century." 2nd ed. National Education Association, 1998.

Cohen, Philip. "Developing Information Literacy," *Education Update* 37.2 (1995): or online <http://www.ascd.org/readingroom/edupdate/1995/1feb.html>.

Didier, E. K. Macklin. *Relationships Between Student Achievement in Reading and Library Media Programs and Personnel.* Diss. University of Michigan, 1982. University Microfilms No. 82-14981.

Ercegovac, Zorana. "Bringing the Library Into the Lab: How Information Literacy Skills Make Better Science Students." *School Library Journal* 49.2 (2003): 52-57.

ERIC Clearinghouse on Handicapped and Gifted Children. *Characteristics and Behaviors of the Gifted.* <http://www.ri.net/gifted_talented/character.html>.

Goals 2000: Educate America Act, H. R. 1804, 103rd Congress, Second Session, January, 25, 1994. <http://www.ed.gov/legislation/GOALS2000/TheAct/>.

Kuhlthau, Carol C., Ed. *Information Literacy: Learning How to Learn*. Chicago: American Library Association, 1991.

Kuhlthau, Carol C. "Information Skills for an Information Society: A Review of Research." (1987) Syracuse, NY: ERIC Clearinghouse on Information Resources. ED 297 740.

Lance, Keith Curry. "Impact of School Library Media Programs on Academic Achievement." *Teacher Librarian* 29.3 (2002): 29-34.

Lance, Keith C., Marcia J. Rodney, and Christine Hamilton-Pennel. *Information Empowered: The School Librarian as an Agent of Academic Achievement in Alaska Schools*. Juneau: St. Lib., 1999.

---. *Measuring Up to Standards: The Impact of School Library Programs and Information Literacy in Pennsylvania Schools*. Camp Hill, PA: PA Citizens for Better Lib., 2000.

Lance, Keith C., Lynda Welborn, and Christine Hamilton-Pennell. *The Impact of School Library Media Centers on Academic Achievement*. Castle Rock, CO: Hi Willow, 1993.

Lyman, Peter, and Hal R. Varian. "How Big Is the Information Explosion?" *IMP Magazine*. Online publication, see <http://www.cisp.org/imp/november_2000/11_00lyman.htm>.

National Forum on Information Literacy. "An Overview." <http://infolit.org/>.

Oberman, C. "Avoiding the Cereal Syndrome, Or, Critical Thinking in the Electronic Environment." *Library Trends* 39 (1991): 189-202.

U.S. Department of Labor. Secretary's Commission on Achieving Necessary Skills. "What Work Requires of Schools: A SCANS Report for America 2000." Washington, D.C.: U.S. Government Printing Office, 1991. ED 332 054.

U.S. National Commission on Excellence in Education. *A Nation at Risk: The Imperative for Educational Reform*. Washington, D.C.: U.S. Government Printing Office, 1983.

U.S. National Commission on Libraries and Information Science (NCLIS). <http://www.nclis.gov/about/mission.html/> and <http://www.nclis.gov/about/25yrrpt.html/>.

## Source for Introductory Quote

American Library Association. Presidential Committee on Information Literacy. "Information Literacy: Final Report, January, 1989" in *Information Literacy: Learning How to Learn*, Carol C. Kuhlthau, Ed. Chicago: American Library Association, 1991: 1.

# 2

# Library Skills to Information Literacy

> We need to be honest about the glittering ideals that standards represent and to get beyond their vagueness into the specifics of everyday actions that make them realizable.
>
> *- Kathleen Roskos et. al*

Today information literacy is taking its place as a recognized area of study; one that is important for all students to master and that relates to every content area. Three library organizations have defined information literacy and established standards for skill instruction: (1) the American Association of School Librarians, (2) the Association for Educational Communications and Technology, and (3) the Association of College and Research Libraries. Other organizations have endorsed the importance of information literacy, and many authors have presented strategies to use in teaching these skills. Yet there is no agreed-upon curriculum for information literacy. So it must be said that information literacy is a work in progress. This chapter investigates instructional models that should be part of an information literacy curriculum. By including them, a library skills curriculum evolves as an information literacy curriculum.

## Definitions of Information Literacy

*Information Power: Building Partnerships for Learning* defines information literacy as "the ability to find and use information," and promotes it as "the keystone of lifelong learning." A citizen who does not know how to analyze, appraise, compare, discriminate, and question what he sees, hears, and reads is woefully unprepared to choose among political candidates, insurance policies, doctors' advice, or advertised products in the marketplace.

Almost anyone nine or older can explain what *literacy* means. Common responses would be "able to read" or "knowing how to read and write." Although both reading and writing are complex skills involving numerous tasks, it would seem unnecessary to specify these tasks in order to define literacy. This situation is not true for information literacy because this area of study has not reached the point where there is general understanding about the skills that should be included. While many library media specialists may not be certain what should be included in a information literacy curriculum, they do realize the traditional library skills are inadequate.

When *Information Power: Building Partnerships for Learning* was published, it accelerated the process of defining information literacy becase it set forth nine standards for student learning (8-9). These standards describe the skills and knowledge a person needs to be considered information literate. Unfortunately, the way the standards are written and organized causes confusion. Despite the title of Chapter 2, only three of the nine standards are classified as "Information Literacy," the other six are classified differently. In an attempt to tie all nine standards together, the words "information literate" are repeated in every standard, making each statement too long and difficult to grasp. Agreeing with the heading for the first three standards, this chapter addresses only the first three standards from the *Information Power* publication. It will make it easier to compare curriculum if the focus of comparison is on the verbs used in various plans.

The verbs used in the first three *Information Power* standards are "access," "evaluate," and "use," defining information literacy as the ability to access, evaluate, and use information. This definition is consistent with the vision statement found on page one in *Information Power*, "Information literacy—the ability to find and use information—is the keystone of lifelong learning" (1). Definitions developed by other library professionals are similar. The ALA Presidential Committee on Information Literacy defined an information literate as one who knows how to "find, evaluate, and use information effectively to solve a particular problem or make a decision" (1). While developing competencies for college and university students, a committee representing the Association of College & Research Libraries (ACRL) defined the term as "an intellectual framework for understanding, finding, evaluating, and using information" (16). An article in *Australian Academic and Research Libraries* by Robert Burnhein states, "To be information literate, a person must be able to recognize when information is needed and have the ability to locate, evaluate and use effectively the needed information" (192).

# Standards for Student Learning, a Recap

*Information Power: Building Partnerships for Learning* provides nine student-learning standards that describe the behavior of an information-literate student (8-9). Analysis of these standards will determine which skills should be included in an information literacy curriculum. Only the first three standards—those categorized as information literacy—will be analyzed. The other six standards are addressed in chapter four as habits of mind.

What skills are needed to use information competently? The answer can be gained by examining related instructional models and analyzing information literacy goals. The outcome is for students to be able to access information, evaluate information, and use information.

# Models Related to Information Literacy

While definitions are useful, a model often helps an individual grasp the scope and depth of an area. There are a number of models that are pertinent to information handling, these include:

- Thinking skills,
- Research skills,
- Study skills, and
- Technology skills.

As with definitions, sometimes people debate the meaning of terms used in a model.

### Thinking Skills Model

Thinking skills relate to information literacy and these models need to be examined. There is some confusion in use of the terms, "problem solving," "decision-making," and "thinking." These terms are often used as though they were equivalent, but Barry Beyer, the guru of critical thinking, maintains they are different. He defines thinking skills as the "... careful, precise, persistent and objective *analysis* of any knowledge claim or belief to *judge* its validity and/or worth" (271). Yet his list of thinking skill characteristics contrast markedly with the model developed by educators in the Oklahoma City Public Schools. It is more like a research model. These two models are shown in Table 2.1.

Table 2.1

# Comparison of Two Thinking Skills Models

| Beyer's Critical Thinking Objectives | Oklahoma City Public Schools (Rankin-Hughes Thinking Skills) |
|---|---|
| | Plan (sense problem, define problem, set goal) |
| Determines the reliability of a source. | Gather information (observe, recall, question) |
| | Organize information (represent, compare, classify, order) |
| Distinguishes between verifiable facts and value claims. Determines the factual accuracy of a statement. Determines the strength of an argument. Detects bias. Identifies unstated assumptions. Identifies ambiguous or equivocal claims or arguments. Recognizes logical inconsistencies or fallacies in a line of reasoning. Distinguishes between warranted or unwarranted claims. Distinguishes relevant from irrelevant information, claims, or reasons. | Analyze information (distinguish & clarify components and attributes, determine accuracy & adequacy of arguments, recognize patterns & relationships, arrange, identify central element) |
| | Extend & expand information (infer, anticipate, discover relevant outside structures restructure) |
| | Synthesize & create information |

Both thinking skills models, as different as they are, fit within information literacy because the objectives address information handling, are useful in lifelong learning, and relate to every content discipline. These three criteria are the basis to use in judging the appropriateness of including objectives in an information literacy curriculum. Before considering other models, consider how thinking skills relate to school curriculum.

A North Carolina school system developed a booklet to help teachers teach thinking skills in the classroom. It shows how these skills can be translated into classroom activities in language arts, social studies, and science. The tasks cited as thinking skills differ from those used by Beyer and Rankin-Hughes, but this only highlights the different opinions about what tasks are thinking skills. Table 2.2 shows how the thinking skill objectives relate to the three core subjects (Wake County 3).

Table 2.2

## Thinking Skills and Core Content

| Thinking Skills | Language Arts | Social Studies | Science |
|---|---|---|---|
| Identifying alternatives | Identifying multiple sources<br><br>Predicting outcomes | Offering alternatives<br><br>Giving supporting data for opinions | Identifying and testing variables |
| Finding relationships | Comparing & contrasting<br><br>Classifying<br><br>Identifying plot | Comparing & contrasting<br><br>Finding patterns | Classifying |
| Generalizing | Inferring main idea<br><br>Drawing conclusions | Generalizing<br><br>Stating opinions | Hypothesizing |

Table 2.3 builds on the relationship of thinking skills to language arts established in the North Carolina document. This author developed questions relevant to a class setting. These questions are as pertinent to information literacy as they are to language arts. These examples should make it evident that incorporating thinking skills into the information literacy curriculum is not really such a big step.

Table 2.3

## Skills as Language Arts Activities

| Identifying alternatives | Finding relationships | Generalizing |
|---|---|---|
| What could be another title for this book? | Is the story historical fiction or historical fantasy? | What was the main idea of the story? |
| How might the story have ended? | Which word was a better match? | Do you think the main character acted in self-defense? |
| What is another source for this kind of information? | How would you compare the main characters in the two plays? | Why is a news digest the quickest way to get the answer? |
| Why did the character react in that manner? | How do the two databases compare and contrast? | Considering the statistics, which state will prosper? |
| How would the story have been different in a different time period? | How does the Dewey Classification System compare to an alphabetical system? | Do you think the parable was relevant? |

### Research Skills Model

Research models have been part of traditional library skill instruction for many years. In fact, some people equate research skills with library literacy. Several research models are familiar to library media specialists: those by Eisenberg and Berkowitz, Kuhlthau, and Stripling and Pitts are probably the best known. These authors address the same outcome, but they use different steps and language to describe the research process. The "Big6" model developed by Eisenberg and Berkowitz is a frequently adapted and adopted model. It includes six steps: (1) task definition, (2) information seeking strategies, (3) location of and access to information, (4) use of information, (5) synthesis, and (6) evaluation (101). Whenever the words "stages" or "steps" are mentioned, they are always followed with a caveat that the words are misleading because the process is not sequential but recursive, meaning it is often necessary to revisit a stage.

To help an individual understand the essence of a skill, focus on the verb that designates the action to be taken. Comparing verbs makes it easier to grasp differences. Table 2.4 compares the verbs used in five information literacy models. One was developed by the Oklahoma City Schools, others are an adaptation of the "Big6" used by the Mankato [MN] schools, the Association of Colleges and Research Libraries model, the *Information Power: Building Partnerships for Learning* model, and a model developed by the state of Wisconsin.

Table 2.4

# Comparison of Information Literacy Models

| OK City | Mankato, MN | AASL/AECT | ACRL | Wisconsin |
|---|---|---|---|---|
| Plan | Task definition | | Determines | |
| Gather | Information seeking Locate Access | Find | Accesses | Locate Select |
| Organize | | | | Organize |
| Analyze Extend Expand Synthesize | Synthesis | | | Synthesize |
| Evaluate | Evaluation | Evaluate | Evaluates | |
| Create Apply | Presentation | Use | Uses | Present |
| | Basic skills* | | Understands** | Enjoy literature |

*Basic skills in this plan include ethical and legal use of information, as well as computer skills.
**Understands is defined as legal, economic, and ethical issues.

The five models differ despite being designed for the same purpose. The models use different language. "Location and retrieval" tasks are evident in all five models. "Evaluate" or "evaluation" appear in four of the five models. "Use" is only found in the AASL/AECT list, but synonyms appear in the others. Comparing verbs and models helps to focus our thinking about information literacy.

## Study Skills Model

There are many study skills and most of them relate to handling information, such as previewing, questioning, underlining, note taking, outlining, and summarizing. Students who have these skills can acquire and use information in an effective and efficient manner. Devine's review of research on study skills instruction found evidence that these skills help students "better understand, remember, and apply knowledge" (743).

Study skills are often taught as a special instructional unit instead of being integrated with regular content instruction. An example is the popular SQ3R (survey, question, read, review, recite) system. Underlining, note taking, mapping, and summarizing are study skills that are usually taught as research skills. Study skills belong in the information literacy curriculum because other information literacy skills are pertinent to every discipline and used in lifelong learning. Study skills need to be practiced to the point they become internalized, which means they need to become habits. For example, if students are taught previewing skills in the early grades and always prompted to preview before reading, they will soon apply those skills without being reminded. Study skills are taught through modeling, direct instruction, practice, and review. Devine (750) suggests students should

- Acquire a range of study skills,
- Understand how they can help in test taking, and
- Understand how performance is helped in all classes.

These suggestions are as relative to information literacy instruction as they are to study skills instruction.

## Technology Skills

In recent years, the formats available for students to share information have multiplied. Traditionally students shared their information in a research paper, but today they can produce a slide presentation, design a web page, make a poster, design a transparency, or make a videotape as often as writing a paper. Students need production competencies if they are going to share information in the most appropriate format.

Computer skills are essential because computers are used to obtain, manage, and share information. Today's students must know how to access digitized information because so much information is only available in digital format. The State Library of Pennsylvania, under Doris Epler's able leadership, recognized the need for students to gain competence in using computer databases. They developed a computer skills model and produced a helpful guide for training students in online searching. Outcomes stated in the Pennsylvania model include:

- Develop the research question,
- Identify key words,
- Expand key words,
- Recognize general and specific topics,
- Choose the most appropriate terms,
- Recognize the relationship between key words, and
- Develop a search strategy (1-2).

This guide is particularly useful in teaching students to choose and combine search terms (11-14). It also offers lessons and worksheets to teach Venn diagrams, logical operators, and positional operators. In the past, Venn diagrams were used mainly in mathematics classes to teach reasoning; however, these diagrams help students learn how to broaden or narrow a search.

Considering how relevant the tasks in these models are to information literacy, it is evident that these skills are broader and more complex than library skills. Next, follow a curriculum development process to see how standards lead to goals that lead to instructional objectives that lead to a teaching plan.

# Curriculum Development

Curriculum or course of study development is a process that moves from generalities to specifics. Standards are the generalities because they are broad statements or goals that represent an ideal condition. A goal or standard does nothing to explain how it can be accomplished. Someone must translate a goal into categories and then into objectives before there is a path that can be followed to achieve the goal. Usually a curriculum committee is composed of selected teachers at a school, or school representatives at the district level, or district representatives working at the state level.

These committees usually begin their work by analyzing existing curricula and comparing them to current standards. Committee members examine current professional literature to determine trends, new content, and emerging practices. Usually a committee moves from setting goals to identifying categories for instruction, and finally to writing instructional objectives that fit within the established categories. The purpose of the curriculum development process is to provide a structure for teachers to use in planning units and lessons. If left alone to interpret and implement standards, many teachers would struggle with the complexities and resort to teaching the textbook page by page.

In some instances a state agency or professional organization prepares an implementation plan when new standards are released. For example, when the first version of *Information Power* was published, a number of agencies and organizations produced documents to help school professionals implement the new guidelines. Illustrative of this type of publication are:

- Alabama Department of Education, *Enriching Education: Information Power for Alabama Students*, 1992
- California Media & Library Educators, *From Library Skills to Information Literacy*, 1993
- New Hampshire Department of Education, *Information Skills,* 1992

Similarly, when the 1998 version of *Information Power* was published that more strongly emphasized information skill instruction, state and professional organizations again responded to the need to translate standards into implementation documents. The Alabama State Department of Education was one such organization. Aided by library media specialists selected from across the state, the agency developed a guide for school library media specialists to use in implementing the new 1998 standards. Contrary to the traditional approach just described, the Alabama committee used a reverse process explained in the next section.

# The Alabama Approach

Usually curriculum development moves from the generalities of goals to the specifics of written objectives; however, Alabama reversed the process. The Alabama committee decided to identify objectives that were already written, being implemented, and tested in classrooms across the state. This decision was made in part because both educators and the public were concerned about poor student performance on required statewide tests and it seemed important to tie information skills to test objectives. A second reason the committee decided to use this approach was to illustrate the relationship of information literacy with academic disciplines.

The curriculum-planning committee began their work by discussing what a student would know and be able to do if he or she were information literate, as described in the nine *Information Power* standards. Next, they examined how the existing information curriculum document related to the nine standards and then examined the courses of study that listed teaching objectives for every required course in grades kindergarten through 12th. Each time they identified an objective pertinent to information handling, it was added to the list of information literacy objectives—at the same grade level where it was included in the course guide. Next, the committee reviewed objectives on which state-mandated tests were based. For example, Alabama requires students to take the Stanford Achievement Test in grades 3-11, a writing assessment in grades 4 and 8, and an exit exam for high school seniors. The test objectives found to address information handling were added to the list for the new curriculum.

There was lengthy and occasionally heated discussion by committee members as they considered each objective because they had different opinions about what information literacy included. Some members had a broader view than others. For example, when members considered a high school objective in which students would learn to create a mnemonic device to use as an aid in recalling specific information, there were many different opinions. Some thought it should be included as an information literacy objective because it addressed information, others thought that it was a study skill objective and did not relate to information literacy. Some thought it should be included simply because it was a standardized test objective. Perhaps this example makes it is easier to understand why it took a calendar year to finish the curriculum guide.

As an organizational strategy, the committee used the action verbs found in the first three student learning standards in *Information Power* (AASL/AECT 8). Table 2.5 represents a page from the final Alabama Department of Education document. On this page, please notice the italics denote a standardized test objective. As you review the sample page try to identify the subject area related to the objective. If this task is difficult, it may underscore the interdisciplinary nature of information literacy. It also adds weight to the principle that the best way to teach these skills is for teachers and media specialists to collaborate in planning instruction and integrating information skills with classroom instruction.

Table 2.5

# Page From *Literacy Partners,* an AL Document

## FIFTH GRADE

| Access | Evaluate | Use |
|---|---|---|
| Use statistical sources to locate and verify figures related to a specific topic. | *Extend meaning of material read, viewed, and/or heard.** | Collaborate with others, using technology to share information. |
| Use geographical sources to locate information about places. | *Identify author techniques that show elapsed time.** | Create a topic-specific database. |
| Use guidewords, keys, and search terms to retrieve information efficiently. | Distinguish among myths, legends, and fables. | Use photography or another visual form to communicate a message. |
| Use cross-references to locate additional information. | Differentiate between figurative and literal language. | Write paragraphs and stories to dramatize a point, experience, or opinion. |
| Extrapolate information from graphs, charts, and tables. | Recognize the use of bias and propaganda. | |
| Read labels for information. | Compare news reports on an event from various sources. | |

*Italics indicate objectives from the standardized test used to test fifth grade students.

# The Mobile [AL] Contribution

When the committee had finished their work, Alabama's library media specialists were pleased to have a curriculum guide for information literacy. However, some of them were uncertain how to translate the curriculum objectives into a teaching program. A committee of library media specialists from the Mobile County Public Schools worked through the summer to develop examples to illustrate how to integrate information literacy into course content. In developing these illustrations, the committee used Alabama's course guide for social studies, which was organized by the following four strands:

- Historic literacy
- Geographic literacy
- Economic literacy
- Civic literacy

The Mobile committee worked diligently and their document has helped many practitioners understand how to move from standards to written objectives and on to a teaching plan. Assessment was the aspect that troubled committee members the most. This does not seem unusual because media specialists receive little training in measurement and evaluation. This is a situation that must change because testing is essential for effective teaching.

Readers will enjoy reviewing the examples developed by the Mobile [AL] library media specialists. These examples illustrate how content objectives and information literacy objectives relate and how they can be translated into learning activities. These pages are provided with the kind permission of the Mobile County Schools.

# HISTORIC LITERACY

**Curriculum Objective(s): #44**
- Assess significant features of the Civil War.

**Information Literacy Objective(s):**
- Retrieve information about a given topic from sources in different formats.
- Extend meaning of material read, viewed, and heard.
- Relate the copyright laws to the use of resources.
- Collaborate with others in using technology to share information.
- Use photography or other visual forms to communicate a message.

**Activities:**
- Students use textbook, library resources, and the Internet to learn about the Battle of Gettysburg, pinpointing its location on a map and date on a timeline.

- Students read the book, *At Gettysburg: Or What a Girl Saw and Heard of the Battle* by Tillie Pierce Alleman and respond to it in letter form, as a Confederate or Union soldier, a civilian, or a family member of a soldier.

- Students create a multimedia presentation using battle photographs of the Civil War photographer Matthew Brady that can be obtained in reference works or the Internet http://www.civil-war.net/.

- Students read the Gettysburg Address and formulate ideas as to why it was delivered at the battlefield site.

**Assessment(s):**
- Rubric for multimedia project
- Teacher guided discussion about Gettysburg

# GEOGRAPHIC LITERACY

**Curriculum Objective(s): #36**
- Discuss migration and trade patterns of Westward Expansion before the Civil War.

**Information Literacy Objective(s):**
- Use geographical sources to locate information about places.
- Retrieve information about a given topic from sources in different formats.
- Extend meaning of material read, viewed, or heard.
- Write paragraphs and stories to illustrate or dramatize a point.

**Activities:**
- Students use textbooks to determine routes of different migrations, then use an atlas to determine at least 20 landmarks the pioneers would have encountered. These can be mountains, particular cities/towns, rivers, forts, etc. Students must list at least two facts about each landmark, and cite the sources used. Students also describe participants of the migrations, describing their origins, beliefs, etc.

- Students use colored pencils to map each trail west on a map of the United States, indicating with symbols the landmarks located on each trail. Students construct a legend for the map.

- Students use *Oregon Trail 11* (CD-ROM) to gain an understanding of different types of geographic terrain the pioneers encountered.

- Students read one book from *The Little House* series by Laura Ingalls Wilder and present a skit for the class that they have adapted from the book.

**Assessment(s):**
- Correctly completed map
- Checklists

# ECONOMIC LITERACY

**Curriculum Objective(s): #8**
- Assess the impact of the Age of Discovery upon European Society.

**Information Literacy Objective(s):**
- Extrapolate information from graphs, charts, and tables.
- Retrieve information about a given topic from sources in different formats.
- Extend meaning of material read, viewed, and heard.
- Recognize the use of bias and propaganda.
- Write paragraphs and stories to illustrate or dramatize a point.

**Activities:**
- Students identify early explorers of North America using library resources and textbooks.

- Students prepare an "Explorer's Notebook" to be presented to the monarchy of their homeland. The notebook will describe people and cultures encountered, plants discovered, precious metals, spices, and other materials deemed valuable.

- Students research the cost of Columbus's expedition, his salary, and his crews' pay, cost of food, ship maintenance, etc. Compare and contrast these figures with the cost of an ocean voyage today by constructing a graph.

- Design a poster to solicit crew members for a New World expedition that includes salary statements and other incentives.

**Assessment(s):**
- Checklists

# POLITICAL LITERACY

**Curriculum Objective(s): #28**
- Discuss the major aspects of the Constitutional Convention.

**Information Literacy Objective(s):**
- Use guidewords, keys, and search terms to retrieve information efficiently.
- Retrieve information about a given topic from sources in different formats.
- Extend meaning of material read, viewed, and heard.
- Write paragraphs and stories to illustrate or dramatize a point.

**Activities:**
- Students read books, *Shh ... We're Writing the Constitution,* by Jean Fritz and *If You Were There When They Signed the Constitution,* by Elizabeth Levy.

- Students brainstorm ideas for creating a classroom constitution, compromising as delegates did at the Constitutional Convention to form an acceptable document.

- Students research the representatives to the Constitutional Convention and present, in chart format, information about at least 10 of the delegates. Information such as home state, profession, and political views must be included.

- Students use reference books to paraphrase the Preamble to the Constitution.

**Assessment(s):**
- Class constitution
- Completed chart of representatives to the Constitutional Convention

Although the approach used by Alabama's media specialists worked for them, it ran contrary to traditional curriculum development. In the next chapter, the author follows a four-stage, curriculum development process to develop an information literacy curriculum.

## In Summary

The aim of this chapter was to energize and focus the reader's thoughts about what information literacy instruction involves. It would be useful to have a consensus across the library media profession. Though there may never be a written, national curriculum or related standardized assessments, such tools would help administrators, teachers, and parents understand what it means to be information literate and could show how these skills improve student performance. A national curriculum could provide consistency to a mobile population where students move frequently from one location to another. It would also provide a basis for sharing information about successful activities targeted to specific objectives rather than just a plethora of ideas in myriad journals and books.

A national curriculum tied to effective assessment measures would make it possible to collect data that could be used to substantiate the contributions and effectiveness of school media services. Tests developed by hundreds of practitioners could form the basis for developing standardized measures. Broad-based assessments could focus added attention on information literacy as an area of study where students need to meet or exceed the national average. When this point is reached, information skills will really be basic skills.

# Sources Cited

Alabama State Department of Education. *Literacy Partners: A Principal's Guide to an Effective Library Media Program for the 21st Century.* Bulletin 46. Montgomery, AL: The Department, 1999.

American Association of School Librarians. Association for Educational Communications and Technology. *Information Power: Building Partnerships for Learning.* Chicago: American Library Association, 1998.

American Library Association. Presidential Committee on Information Literacy. "Information Literacy: Final Report, January, 1989" in *Information Literacy: Learning How to Learn*, Carol C. Kuhlthau, Ed. Chicago: American Library Association, 1991: 1-8.

Association of College and Research Libraries. "Information Literacy: Competency Standards for Higher Education." *Teacher Librarian* 28.3 (2001): 16-22.

Beyer, Barry K. "Critical Thinking: What Is It?" *Social Education* 49.4 (1985): 270-276.

Burnhein, Robert. "Information Literacy—A Core Competency." *Australian Academic and Research Libraries* 23.4 (1999): 188-96.

Devine, Thomas G. *Teaching Study Skills: A Guide for Teachers.* Boston: Allyn, 1987.

Eisenberg, Michael B., and Robert E. Berkowitz. *Curriculum Initiative: An Agenda and Strategy for Library Media Programs.* Norwood, NJ: Ablex, 1990.

Eisenberg, Michael B., and Robert E. Berkowitz. *Resource Companion to Curriculum Initiative: An Agenda and Strategy for Library Media Programs.* Norwood, NJ: Ablex, 1988.

"Information Literacy: Final Report, January, 1989." in *Information Literacy: Learning How to Learn*. Chicago: American Library Association, (1991): 1-8.

Kuhlthau, Carol C. *Teaching the Library Research Process: A Step-by-Step Approach for Secondary Schools.* Englewood Cliffs, NJ: The Center for Applied Research in Education, 1985.

Mankato [MN] Schools Information Literacy Curriculum Guidelines, <http://www.isd77.k12.mn.us/resources/infocurr/infolit.html>.

Mobile County Public Schools. "Collaborative Designs for Information Literacy." Mobile, AL: Mobile County Public Schools, 1999: 29-30. Loose-leaf binder.

Oklahoma State Department of Education. *Information Skills: Suggested Learner Outcomes, Grades K-12*. Oklahoma City: The Department, 1987.

Stanford Achievement Test Series. 9th ed. *Compendium Supplement*. Harcourt Brace Educational Measurement, n.d.

State Library of Pennsylvania, *Problem Definition Process: A Guide to Research Strategies*. Harrisburg, PA: Pennsylvania Department of Education, 1989.

Stripling, Barbara K., and Judy M. Pitts. *Brainstorms and Blueprints: Teaching Library Research as a Thinking Process*. Englewood, CO: Libraries Unlimited, 1988.

Wake County Public School System. "Interdisciplinary Approach to Teaching Thinking Skills Through Language." ESEA Title II-B Basic Skills Improvement Project, 1981.

Wisconsin Dept. of Public Instruction. *Matrix for Curriculum Planning in Library Media and Information Skills*. Madison: The Department, 1989.

## Source for Introductory Quote

Roskos, Kathleen, Victoria J. Risko, et al. "Head, Heart, and the Practice of Literacy Pedagogy." *Reading Research Quarterly* 33.2 (1998): 228-240.

# 3

# Information Literacy Curriculum: A Traditional Approach

> Just as meaning is not contained in the text on a page, literacy cannot be found in the ability to decipher those texts, but in the habits and strengths needed to create meanings and to challenge foolishness—on the page, from the lips of others, and from individuals themselves.
>
> *- Richard Kearns and Linda Bannister*

## From Generalities to Specifics

In this chapter the author follows a traditional approach to develop an information literacy curriculum. Traditionally, the process begins with a curriculum committee discussing what a student should know and be able to do with the subject after thirteen years of study. The committee's decisions provide the goals for curriculum development. For the curriculum proposed in this chapter, goals were drawn from *Information Power: Building Partnerships for Learning*. These goals charge library media specialists with assisting students in becoming:

- Active and creative locators,
- Evaluators, and
- Users of information to solve problems and to satisfy their own curiosity (2).

However, this author decided to use access (because access is broader than locate), evaluate, and use as goals for a proposed information literacy curriculum. As a result, the proposed curriculum ensures students can access, evaluate, and use information. Next, these goals are analyzed to determine the skills and knowledge they require.

# Analyze Goals to Determine the Elements of Instruction

Once goals are set, it is necessary to analyze each goal to determine the knowledge and skills required to reach it. Analysis requires thinking through the actions and considerations an individual takes when accessing, evaluating, and using information.

*Access* involves more than just location and retrieval. Before a person can access information, he must determine the type of information needed, assess the amount of information required, specify plausible sources, and know the scope and arrangement of each source. The more sources a person knows, the greater the likelihood of a successful search. So *assessing* need comes before *accessing* information.

These two procedures require different skills and bodies of knowledge. Assessing need requires appraising, estimating, questioning, hypothesizing, and judging relevance. Accessing requires knowing various resources, their locations, and organization. Enabling skills that make information seeking more efficient, such as the use of guidewords, cross-references, and search terms, are also important.

*Evaluate* is a critically important skill that is used throughout the information handling process. Helping students develop evaluation skills is harder than teaching them how to access materials because there are so many facets to consider. A student must learn to evaluate whether or not the information is appropriate, adequate, accurate, current, and free from bias. These tasks require critical thinking. As the information consumed by a student becomes more mature and complex, his evaluation skill must become more sophisticated.

*Use of information* after it is accessed and found adequate, can be for study or pleasure. Although this point was made earlier, it bears repeating, there are two distinct interpretations of the term, "use." Before a student can use information to produce a paper, presentation, or product, it must be interpreted and organized. Interpretation involves deriving meaning, comparing, contrasting, translating and explaining. Organization involves summarizing, categorizing, and arranging systematically. In addition to traditional library skills, it is clear an information literacy curriculum should include thinking skills, production skills, study skills, and technology skills.

Equipment and computer-operation skills are not included in the proposed curriculum, which might cause some raised eyebrows, although there is logic behind the omission. If you consider equipment operation as skills needed to procure information from various formats, then these skills seem essential. However, if you draw a parallel between equipment-operation skills and reading skills, which are necessary to gain information from the printed page, then it seems unnecessary to specify them in the curriculum. It is assumed a student must be able to read in order to acquire printed information or operate equipment to obtain information from audiovisual or digital formats. Although a library media specialist might be involved in teaching students to operate equipment, this should not be integral to an information literacy curriculum. Today many students know how to operate computers and other audiovisual equipment before they begin school and this trend is likely to continue or increase. Table 3.1 shows the competencies needed to reach each of the three goals.

Table 3.1

# Elements of Instruction by Goal

**Access**
- Questioning the need for information
- Hypothesizing about possible sources
- Identifying alternative search strategies
- Locating specific information aided by guidewords, tables of content, indexes, book parts, keys, newspaper sections, cross-references, entry points, classification systems, headings, captions, signs, and labels
- Recognizing various types of information (e.g., words, facts, concepts, theories)
- Knowing information formats (e.g., globes, atlases, thesaurus, atlas, almanac)
- Distinguishing fictional formats (e.g., historical fiction, science fiction, fantasy, poetry, etc.)
- Interviewing
- Reading graphs, charts, and other graphical organizers

**Evaluate**
- Previewing
- Scanning and skimming materials
- Estimating
- Using context to determine meaning
- Interpreting the mood, sequence, and setting of a selection
- Judging relevance, timeliness, completeness, accuracy
- Finding relationships (compare & contrast, categorize, generalize, cause & effect)
- Detecting bias
- Identifying errors, inconsistencies, and flawed argument
- Verifying information

**Use**
- Relating new information to what is known
- Note taking and underlining
- Outlining, mapping, and categorizing
- Generalizing
- Inferring and extrapolating
- Creating analogies and metaphors
- Concluding and proving
- Summarizing
- Interpreting and transposing
- Producing
- Writing
- Illustrating

# Designate a Structure for the Curriculum Plan

A plan of organization must be devised as a structure for the elements of instruction. An organizational plan groups similar things together and helps others grasp the plan. Curriculum can be organized by areas, strands, categories, classes, or divisions. Eight categories were selected to organize the curriculum proposed in this chapter. They are:

- Types of information,
- Information sources,
- Information symbols,
- Graphical information,
- Information elements,
- Organization of information,
- Information products, and
- Information issues.

Table 3.2 illustrates the relationship of the three goals of the information literacy curriculum to the eight categories. "Habits of Mind," shown as infiltrating the curriculum, is addressed in the next chapter.

Table 3.2

## Eight Categories for Instruction

| Goals | Eight Categories | | | |
|---|---|---|---|---|
| **ACCESS** | Types of Information | Information Sources | Information Symbols | Graphical Information |
| | | | | |
| **EVALUATE** | Information Elements | | | |
| | | | | |
| **USE** | Organization of Information | Information Products | Information Issues | |
| | *Habits of Mind* | *Habits of Mind* | *Habits of Mind* | *Habits of Mind* |

The eight categories shown in Table 3.2 must be analyzed to identify instructional elements. Table 3.3 shows this analysis.

Table 3.3

## Instructional Elements by Category

| Categories | Elements of Instruction |
|---|---|
| Types of Information | Words, terms, expressions, quotations, foreign phrases, place names, initialisms, acronyms, abbreviations, facts, locations, concepts, laws, statistics |
| Information Sources | Dictionary, glossary, special dictionary, language dictionary, handbook, atlas, globe, map, manual, encyclopedia, fiction, nonfiction, Internet, original document, schedules |
| Information Elements | Main idea, sequence, conclusion, book parts, figurative language, story elements, guide words, newspaper sections, cross reference, labels, search terms, comparison, contrast, metaphor, dialect, citation, footnote |
| Information Symbols | Dewey Decimal System, map symbols, scales, keys, statistics |
| Organization of Information | Alphabetical order, catalog, directory, database, classification, index, content table, Boolean operators, electronic address, search engine |
| Graphical Information | Picture, map, graph, chart, ad, photo, grid |
| Information Products | Picture, chart, graph, timeline, outline, diagram, diorama, story, report, play, pantomime, notes, bibliography, map, web, essay, slide, transparency |
| Information Issues | Care of resources, bias, propaganda, copyright, plagiarism, intellectual freedom |

# Relate Instructional Elements to School Emphases

In order to teach the instructional elements shown in Table 3.3, they need to be arranged in a useable and sensible plan that guides practitioners in curriculum implementation. The implementation plan is usually a grade-by-grade arrangement of skills or topics. Although many elements may be taught in more than one grade, they should be placed at the grade where students learn similar information. This approach provides students with practice opportunities. It is more efficient for students to learn information skills when they can be practiced using classroom content. A review of school curriculum, determined school emphases to be

- Primary grades (K-2) emphasize development of basic skills and learning to get along with others.
- Intermediate grades (3-5) emphasize learning to work independently and applying basic skills.
- Middle grades (6-8) stress group work, problem solving, and gaining knowledge of the wider world.
- Secondary schools (9-12) concentrate on courses that prepare students for college or the workplace.

It is possible to match information literacy skills with each school level's emphasis. Story elements and vocabulary development are emphasized during the primary grades because children are engrossed in learning to read. At this time in their young lives they need to be immersed in stories. Hearing stories read or told helps youngsters learn about story elements and construction. Story tellers help young children learn how to recognize sounds, describe characters, identify settings, understand plots, and remember details. Listening activities help them develop vocabulary, recognize letter sounds, and hear rhymes. The primary grades are appropriate to learn about dictionaries, even if the experience is only seeing a teacher model dictionary use.

In the intermediate grades, students engage in research in both language arts and science, so it is important for these students to learn where and how to find information. They need to use multiple resources when they search and to learn to give credit for borrowed information. Searching for information continues as an emphasis in middle schools but the focus shifts to the use of electronic sources and to sharing information in various modes.

High schools feature academic disciplines or preparing for work, so secondary school students use sophisticated reference sources to locate literary criticism, to define technical language, and to determine current law. At this stage, using original documents is key, but so is using current events sources, government-generated documents, and statistical databases.

## Translate Instructional Elements into Stated Objectives

After instructional elements are specified, organized, and matched to school levels, the instructional elements need to be stated as instructional objectives. While it is not necessary to write objectives that meet the rigid requirements of an instructional designer, an objective should express clearly the intent of instruction and should suggest a way to assess learning. Which of the following objectives contains both elements needed in a stated objective?

- To recognize a call number
- To demonstrate how a call number is used to locate a specific library item.

The second objective suggests how the objective could be tested. To recognize a call number does not identify the true intent of the objective. It might imply that a student, given three or four different symbols, would be able to select the one that was a call number. Obviously, this is not the intent of the objective.

Do not confuse instructional objectives with an activity. An objective states an instructional outcome; an activity is a way to teach an objective. An activity is a one-time event, even if the event occurs over several days, but one objective can spawn many activities. The two examples that follow should clarify the difference between an objective and an activity.

- The student will prepare a bibliography. **[activity]**
- The student using an appropriate format, credits the work of others. **[objective]**

- The student will create a timeline to illustrate events in World War II. **[activity]**
- The student organizes information in chronological order. **[objective]**

Each instructional element must be written as an instructional objective. Next, the instructional objectives must be listed by instructional categories, and then in a grade by grade arrangement.

Armed with a curriculum plan, a media specialist is ready to implement a program to ensure students become information literate. Just as the devil is in the details, however, the true worth of any curriculum plan is in the implementation details.

Three brief notes about curriculum. First, most curricular plans provide a spiral that broadens and deepens throughout the grades. Skills are re-taught, practiced, and extended as a student moves to a higher grade or to a new setting. Repetition is part of effective curricular planning and implementation. In information literacy instruction, repetition is more complex than in many subjects because the information sources and retrieval procedures constantly change, a situation likely to continue for the foreseeable future.

Second, a curriculum plan is never finished. Work may cease on a particular document, but change is constant and the curriculum will change too. Professionals need to expect and, if possible, embrace change.

Third, library media specialists need a curriculum plan, but some of them work in places where there is not one. This chapter's curriculum can be used or adapted by a library media specialist who wants to implement the standards put forth in *Information Power: Building Partnerships for Learning*.

This proposed curriculum is intended to spawn professional discussion. Certainly there will be differences of opinion about which objectives should or should not be listed, or about why they were listed at a certain grade level. Such discussion is welcomed and encouraged because it may serve to accelerate development of a national curriculum for information literacy and standardized assessments. At least, having a curriculum document for information literacy provides opportunities to:

- Connect with classroom teachers,
- Provide students with skills that enable them to perform better academically, and
- Convince administrators that media programs improve school performance.

# Instructional Objectives by Category

## *Types of Information*
- Distinguish fact from fiction.
- Distinguish among various types of fiction.
- Distinguish relevant from irrelevant information.
- Distinguish fact from opinion and recognize point of view in a speech.
- Compare a current event to similar events in the past.

### Information Sources

- Identify information resources that can be found in a library or media center.
- Explain where certain materials are located.
- Use a dictionary to locate information about people, places, and things.
- Use a dictionary to determine word spelling, pronunciation, and meaning.
- Use a dictionary to determine word form, synonyms, and antonyms.
- Use an encyclopedia to locate facts about people, places, and things.
- Identify places using globes and maps.
- Use newspapers and other current event sources to locate information.
- Use a thesaurus to identify the most precise word.
- Use glossaries, special dictionaries, and place-name handbooks to locate information.
- Use an almanac to locate statistics related to a topic or place.
- Use an historical atlas to retrieve information.
- Locate a quotation or poem related to a specific topic.
- Identify the meaning of foreign, archaic, and technical terms.
- Retrieve and evaluate consumer information.
- Search for information using digitized resources.
- Compare search engines and Internet directories.
- Locate government-sponsored information related to specific topics.
- Locate original documents related to a specific topic.
- Identify information on a specific topic from a government agency.
- Locate information related to colleges, universities, or job training.
- Extrapolate and interpolate information collected by local, state, and federal governments.

### Graphical Information

- Retrieve information from grids, schedules, and tables.
- Analyze a political map.
- Locate and extrapolate statistical information given in charts and tables.
- Locate occupational statistics collected by state and federal governments.

### Information Products

- Describe a picture and explain how it relates to the story.
- Create a picture related to a certain story.
- Dramatize stories through acting, pantomime, and puppets.
- Interpret newspaper information.
- Classify information according to a common characteristic.
- Relate information on a topic from more than two sources.
- Create a chart, graph, or table to present information.
- Outline information retrieved from a source.
- Compare information from three sources and cite the sources.
- Compare various news accounts about an incident.
- Create grids, schedules, and tables to relay information.
- Create graphic representations to convey information.
- Revise a Venn diagram to illustrate a better search strategy.

- Compare and contrast ads for similar products.
- Develop a list of authorities on a specific topic.
- Create a product that persuades or sways opinion.

## Information Issues

- Demonstrate proper use of materials.
- Give credit for information used.
- Recognize bias and propaganda.
- Explain the importance of copyright law and intellectual freedom.
- Explain why information should be used in an ethical manner.

## Information Elements

- Make sounds related to specific characters.
- Describe characters in a story.
- Recall words or phrases repeated in a story.
- Identify story elements (setting, characters, main idea, details).
- Recognize implied but not explicitly stated information in a story.
- Recognize dialect and figurative language used in a passage.
- Identify information missing from a search.
- Interpret the meaning of morals, sayings, and maxims.
- Recognize flawed argument in a publication or presentation.
- Use underlining, margin notes, and highlighting to note important information.
- Evaluate the use of slang, dialect, imagery, and dialogue in a novel.
- Illustrate how metaphor and simile are used to explain relationships.
- Recognize and appreciate the use of literary elements and devices.

## Information Symbols

- Recognize how the letters of the alphabet relate to words and stories.
- Use map keys to gather geographical information.
- Demonstrate how alphabetical order is used to organize information and resources.
- Demonstrate how alphanumerical order is used to organize information and resources.
- Use the Dewey Decimal System to locate specific resources.

## Organization of Information

- Tell what happened in a story.
- Predict the ending of a story and suggest a different ending.
- Retell a story in correct sequence.
- Retell a story including details about the characters, setting, and plot.
- Use tables of content and indexes to locate specific information in a book.
- Identify organizational systems used in libraries and media centers.
- Use the library catalog as a location guide.
- Use guidewords and directories to locate information quickly.
- Develop a simple strategy to search for information.
- Refine a search strategy.

- Demonstrate how to broaden and narrow a search using Boolean operators.
- Use parallel construction when developing an outline or chart.
- Generalize information drawn from printed and digital sources.
- Use a style manual as a writing guide.
- Summarize and analyze a speech.

# Instructional Objectives by Grade

*K-2 Program Emphases—Concept of libraries, story elements, sounds and words, beginning reference sources*

### Kindergarten
- Demonstrate proper use of materials.
- Recognize how the letters of the alphabet relate to words and stories.
- Describe a picture and explain how it relates to the story.
- Tell what happened in a story.
- Make sounds related to specific pictures or characters.
- Describe characters in a story.
- Recall words or phrases repeated in a story.
- Create a picture related to a certain story.

### First Grade
- Identify information resources that can be found in a library or media center.
- Explain where certain materials are located.
- Demonstrate how alphabetical order is used to organize things.
- Identify the elements in a story (setting, characters, main idea, details).
- Predict the ending of a story and suggest a different ending.
- Retell a story in correct sequence.
- Distinguish fact from fiction.
- Use a dictionary to locate information about people, places, and things.

### Second Grade
- Retell a story including details about the characters, setting, and plot.
- Recognize implied but not explicitly stated information in a story.
- Dramatize stories by acting, pantomime, and puppets.
- Use a dictionary to determine spelling, pronunciation, and meaning of a word.
- Use an encyclopedia to locate facts about people, places, and things.
- Use tables of content and indexes to locate specific information in a book.
- Interpret newspaper information.
- Identify the purpose of globes and maps.

*Grades 3-5 Program Emphases—Printed and disk information sources, location aids, research process*

## Third Grade

- Identify organizational systems used in libraries and media centers.
- Use the library catalog as a location guide.
- Use map keys, globes, and maps to locate specific geographical information.
- Use guidewords and directories to locate information quickly.
- Classify information according to a common characteristic.
- Relate information on a topic from more than two sources.
- Use newspapers and other current event sources to locate information.
- Create a chart, graph, or table to present information.

## Fourth Grade

- Develop a simple strategy to search for information.
- Formulate questions.
- Summarize information from written passages.
- Give credit for information found.
- Use a dictionary to determine word form, synonyms & antonyms, use.
- Recognize dialect and figurative language used in a passage.
- Distinguish among various types of fiction.
- Recognize bias and propaganda in materials.

## Fifth Grade

- Use a thesaurus to identify the most precise word.
- Search for information using digitized resources.
- Use glossaries, special dictionaries, and place-name handbooks.
- Use an almanac to locate statistics related to a topic or place.
- Use an historical atlas to retrieve information.
- Outline information retrieved from several sources.
- Compare information from three sources and document the sources.
- Compare various news accounts about an incident.

*Grades 6-8 Program Emphases—Electronic research, current events*

## Sixth Grade

- Refine a search strategy.
- Identify information missing from a search.
- Distinguish relevant from irrelevant information.
- Locate a quotation or poem related to a specific topic.
- Identify the meaning of foreign phrases, abbreviations, and acronyms.
- Interpret the meaning of morals, sayings, and maxims.
- Retrieve information from grids, schedules, and tables.
- Create grids, schedules, and tables to relay information.

### Seventh Grade

- Use the Internet to locate a specific type of information.
- Recognize flawed argument in a publication or presentation.
- Create graphic representations to convey information.
- Explain the importance of copyright law and intellectual freedom.
- Revise a Venn diagram to illustrate a better search strategy.
- Demonstrate how to broaden and narrow a search using Boolean operators.
- Use parallel construction when developing an outline or chart.

### Eighth Grade

- Generalize information drawn from printed and digital sources.
- Identify the meaning of foreign, archaic and technical terms.
- Retrieve and evaluate consumer information.
- Compare and contrast ads for similar products.
- Compare search engines and Internet directories.
- Use underlining, margin notes, and highlighting to note important information.

*Grades 9-12 Program Emphases—Subject disciplines, government information, college and business information*

### Ninth Grade

- Locate government-sponsored information related to a specific topic.
- Locate original documents related to a specific topic.
- Analyze a political map.
- Locate and extrapolate statistical information related to a specific topic.
- Evaluate the use of slang, dialect, imagery, and dialogue in a novel.
- Develop a list of authorities on a specific topic.
- Create a multimedia presentation that informs.

### Tenth Grade

- Identify information on a specific topic from a governmental agency.
- Use a style manual as a writing guide.
- Summarize and analyze a speech.
- Explain why information should be used in an ethical manner.
- Use the file transfer protocol (FTP) to obtain information.
- Create a product that convinces or sways opinion.

### Eleventh Grade

- Distinguish fact from opinion and recognize point of view in a speech.
- Locate occupational statistics collected by state and federal governments.
- Locate information related to colleges, universities, or job training.
- Illustrate how metaphor and simile are used to explain relationships.
- Compare biographical information found in information sources and nonfiction books.

### Twelfth Grade
- Recognize and appreciate the use of literary elements and devices.
- Locate financial and business information collected by the federal government.
- Compare a current event to similar events in the past.
- Extrapolate and interpolate information collected by local, state, and federal governments.

## Sources Cited

American Association of School Librarians. Association for Educational Communications and Technology. *Information Power: Building Partnerships for Learning.* Chicago: American Library Association, 1998.

Stanford Achievement Test Series, 9th ed., *Compendium Supplement.* Harcourt Brace Educational Measurement, n.d.

## Source for Introductory Quote

Kearns, Richard, and Linda Bannister. Paper presented at the 40th Annual Meeting of the Conference on College Composition and Communication. Seattle, WA. March 16-18, 1989. [Abstract.] ED 303 806.

# 4

# Habits of Mind

> ... the purpose of education is not in keeping school but in pushing out into the world young citizens who are soaked in habits of thoughtfulness and reflectiveness, joy, and commitment.
>
> *- Debbie Meier*

Two people ride down the road listening to the car radio when a news report comes on the air. One hears the report and begins to wonder about the details, thinking about questions that remain unanswered. Voicing these questions astounds her companion who wonders why she wants to know more. Laughing, she repeats the motto of a grocery-store tabloid, "inquiring minds want to know." An individual with an inquiring but skeptical mind is one with habits of mind.

These habits are mostly mental manipulations involving information. They are practices we use to make information that is received more understandable, manageable, and useful. They are practices an individual takes to clarify or verify information, such as the habit of looking at a map for directions instead of following a hunch. A person with habits of mind is an individual who imagines and hypothesizes about the why and how of things, but it is also an individual who is cautious about accepting information without documentation. A person with habits of mind is one who seeks meaning by connecting new information with previous knowledge through analogy, comparison, and categorization.

Habits of mind may come naturally to gifted learners, but anyone can acquire them. Doing so requires direct teaching and extensive practice until they become routine. The best way to ensure students acquire habits of mind is for every teacher to:

- Stress their importance,
- Model their use,
- Teach them directly, and
- Provide many opportunities for students to apply them.

When students repeat information handling practices as part of daily instruction, they become internalized as habits of mind.

# Habits of Mind and Science Standards

The term, habits of mind, gained attention when *Science for All Americans* was published in 1989. This document recommended what students should know and be able to do in science by the time they graduated from high school. It was a forerunner to the science standards document, *Benchmarks for Science Literacy*. When science teachers use "habits of mind," they are describing the mindset of a scientist at work. In essence, a scientist's mindset is a person with a questioning but skeptical attitude, and a person who seeks to verify the ideas and opinions offered by others. This is also an apt description of an information literate person. Therefore, it seems appropriate to borrow the term and concept from science education and apply it to information literacy.

*Science for All Americans* lists five categories to describe the habits of mind that scientists routinely use in their work. Those categories are

- *Values and attitudes,*
- Computation and estimation,
- Manipulation and observation,
- *Communication skills*, and
- *Critical-response skills.*

The categories in italics are similar to areas of information literacy because they address standards four through nine of the Standards for Student Learning in *Information Power: Building Partnerships for Learning*. Those six standards address using information in independent learning and in a socially responsible manner. The following sections examine the categories in the science document and show how they relate to information literacy.

## Values and Attitudes

The science standards stress the importance of teachers helping students understand established societal values yet be open to change when new information calls those values into question. Instead of accepting things on face value, students must learn to question and seek verification. Knowledge must shape their opinions instead of going along with the crowd. Scientists reflect three attitudes:

- Curiosity,
- Openness to new ideas, and
- Informed skepticism (4).

For students to develop these attitudes, teachers must encourage their natural curiosity yet model how to resist impulsiveness and embracing every idea. A beginner is prone to accept the first answer, but as he has experience, he will become selective, realizing some answers are better than others. The purpose of instruction and practice is for every student to be curious, open-minded, and truth-seeking.

The "Social Responsibility" standards in the library media guidelines are similar to the values and attitudes described in the science guide because they address the legal and ethical use of information. Using information in an ethical manner is more a matter of attitude than skill, so educators need to model this behavior constantly. When students see teachers and other adults giving credit for borrowed ideas and valuing different points of view, they will behave similarly. Getting students to this point, however, requires thought, time, planning, and repetition on an instructor's part. Repetition is essential to the formation of a habit.

## Communication Skills

Good communication skills are key to success in any discipline or endeavor. The ability to receive, interpret, and deliver information effectively in various modes is as important to information literacy as it is for science literacy. *Science for All Americans* stresses the importance of "fidelity and clarity" in communication (12). Being truthful and clear when communicating means checking the information. Students frequently begin sharing their work before verifying and editing it. Instructors who allow this practice limit student progress.

Science standards also stress the importance of using graphic formats to share information because this type of information is more readily grasped by others. Clarity in presentation is not adequate if the information is inaccurate. Information must be verified and summarized before it appears in a chart or graph. Communication skills may be science skills, but they are also information literacy skills.

## Critical Response Skills

There are two facets to critical response skills. One facet is being able to fairly judge the works of others, and the second facet is being able to judge one's own work. The evaluation skills are similar, but require a different level of self-confidence. While individuals tend to be more critical of their own work than they are of others' work, they may find it difficult to accept constructive criticism from others. When students have feelings of self-worth and self-confidence, they find it easier to accept criticism. Having rubrics to guide their appraisals, helps them fairly critique the work of others. Modeling helps students spot prejudice, faulty arguments, and inaccuracies. Critical response skills are not developed in a day; learning them requires frequent modeling and repeated practice.

If students develop habits of mind, how will it help them learn more in class and perform better on tests? According to the science document, they will be curious, will persevere, will be open minded, given to reflection, and respectful of evidence (Habits 1). A student who has developed habits of mind will

- Value learning,
- Stay on task,
- Adjust when something doesn't work,
- Consider alternatives,
- Use personal strengths, and
- Accept responsibility.

A student who engages frequently in posing questions, seeking answers and alternatives, and verifying data will be better at solving problems and thinking creatively. Whether learning science or information literacy, these are powerful practices.

# Comparing Science Research and Information Research

Science research and information literacy research follow similar procedures. A science teacher wants students to observe, raise questions about things that happen in the natural world, and try to find answers to those questions through experiments. Similarly, a media specialist wants students to trace a topic, analyze a report, raise questions about the information it contains, and locate corroborating information. Stated outcomes are to hypothesize, to collect, and to verify. Both instructors want to encourage data collection, but temper acceptance with skepticism until the results are checked. A science teacher expects students to keep accurate records about results of the experiment and ideas borrowed from others. A media specialist expects students to accurately cite where they borrowed information. In the comparison that follows, Eisenberg and Berkowitz's "Big6" model represents the library research process.

| Stages in the Scientific Process | The "Big6" Research Stages |
| --- | --- |
| Observe and ask questions | Task Definition |
| Form a hypothesis | Information Seeking Strategies |
| Plan an experiment | Location and Access |
| Conduct the experiment | Use of Information |
| Draw conclusions | Synthesis |
| Communicate results | Evaluation |

Whether studying science or information literacy, students must learn to hypothesize, question, locate information, record information or data, classify, compare, infer, summarize, interpolate, and extrapolate. An instructor's goal when teaching either research process should be for students to internalize it so they proceed through habit, not needing a model to follow.

## Teaching Habits of Mind

Children need to start developing habits of mind even before they begin school. Parents can help encourage a child's natural curiosity by helping him wonder about things. Some parents fail to foster curiosity by ignoring their children's questions. Yet a curious child can develop into a questioning adult who constantly wants to know more—a habit that promotes lifelong learning. Parents can foster their child's performance by modeling how to pose pertinent questions, a practice that can begin when reading stories to young children. A parent might read the name of the story and question why it has that title.

A booklet available from ERIC, *What Should Parents Know About Information Literacy*, suggests actions for parents to take in order to help their children develop information skills. The suggestions include:

- Encourage, support, and guide your children in exploring their interests.
- Use "The Big Six" to help your children with their homework.
- Show your children how to evaluate information.
- Teach your children about authors.
- Instruct your children to consider the reliability of information from the Internet.
- Discuss information literacy with your children's teachers.

A system-wide approach is the best way to ensure school-age students to develop habits of mind. When faculty members work together and agree these habits are important, students will acquire them. A practice taught once and only reviewed from time to time will not become a habit. For students to internalize these habits, they must be taught, practiced extensively, and applied to every subject throughout the school year, every year. There must be a plan to develop these habits, but faculty members must also be alert to incidental opportunities.

Checking for accuracy is an important habit for students to develop. One way to develop this habit is for students to routinely use a dictionary instead of guessing about meaning or spelling. This habit can develop in primary years through daily practice, and extend through the twelfth grade. Kindergarten teachers can model use of a dictionary each time a new word appears in a story being read. She might wonder aloud about the meaning of the word, look for clues in the story or illustration, but to be certain about the meaning she would consult a dictionary. As she uses the dictionary, she reminds students how it is organized, letting those that can help sound the letters until the appropriate section is found. A first grade teacher demonstrates an interest in the different types of information a dictionary contains about a word and models how each type is useful. Second grade students use picture dictionaries and student dictionaries to locate meaning of unknown words or find out how to spell words they recognize but cannot spell. Routinely consulting word sources for verification and clarification continues through all grades if there is a plan. Table 4.1 illustrates how a plan might look to teach students use of vocabulary resources.

Table 4.1

# A Scope and Sequence for the Study of Vocabulary

| Kindergarten | Words to label pictures<br>Words related to text |
|---|---|
| Grade 1 | Dictionary arrangement, picture dictionary |
| Grade 2 | Primary dictionary for spelling and meaning |
| Grade 3 | Telephone directory, thesaurus, guide words |
| Grade 4 | Search terms, place names, pronunciation keys, multiple meanings |
| Grade 5 | Glossaries, special dictionaries, most precise word |
| Grade 6 | Quotation, Internet search terms |
| Grade 7 | Parallel construction |
| Grade 8 | Foreign and archaic words, geographic and technical terms, mnemonic devices |
| Grade 9 | Museums, symbols, info systems, slang, dialect |
| Grade 10 | History of words, initialisms, literary devices |
| Grade 11 | Slogan, maxims, imagery, analogies |
| Grade 12 | Causes for language change |

Table 4.2

# Relationship of School Emphases to Information Literacy and Habits of Mind

| Grade Level | School Emphases | Information Literacy | Habits of Mind |
|---|---|---|---|
| **Primary** | Basic skills<br>Working together | Fiction elements<br>Words | Dictionary use<br>Word elements |
| **Intermediate** | Application of skills (science projects)<br>Community, World | Research process<br>Print-based reference tools | Previewing<br>Note-taking<br>Summarizing<br>Inferring |
| **Middle** | Exploration<br>Social concerns | Electronic searches<br>Mass media | Information organization<br>Cue words |
| **Secondary** | Subject dominance<br>Career preparation | Original documents<br>Subject-specific tools | Analysis<br>Evaluation<br>Bias |

Table 4.2 broadens information presented in Table 4.1 to illustrate how information literacy habits relate to concepts taught at each school level.

Students must learn to evaluate their own work with a critical eye and to be open to the work of others. Several activities show how these habits can be developed in the high school. A student's written report is projected on the screen from a laptop computer for other students to critique his work, using a rubric they had devised earlier. A student shares a first-hand account of life during the Great Depression as written in the diary of a former town mayor. In the library media center, a group of students develop a computerized slide presentation to illustrate how pollution affects the local community. To acquire current information and to make certain their report conforms to accepted measures, the students consulted with state and national agencies through e-mail. A second group edits a printed document to accompany the slide presentation when it is shown at the next city council meeting. One student videotapes the performance of the two students chosen to make the presentation, while several students evaluate the presentation and make suggestions for improvement. A fourth group uses electronic databases and e-mail to research actions taken by other communities to solve pollution problems. These students are developing habits of sharing, checking, and critiquing information.

Students must learn to preview material before starting to read. They determine the organizational strategy used by the author or authors so the material can be covered quickly, yet thoroughly. After reading the information, they check to see if it is up-to-date by using current databases, especially investigating any statistics presented. They locate information about the author to determine his credentials and conjecture how his background might have influenced his interest in the topic. They notice the sources that are cited to see where additional information can be found when these things are done without direction from the teacher, the students have developed habits of mind.

## Developing Good Habits

To develop good habits, students need numerous opportunities to practice how information is organized and to identify important elements. Divesta, Hayward, and Orlando explain that gifted learners innately handle information in a proficient manner (99), but teachers and media specialists can help all students develop these habits.

The following scenario illustrates how students can practice good habits while simultaneously helping the teacher.

The teacher will begin a new social studies unit in two weeks and wants to be prepared so maximum time can be spent on instruction. Each day when school is dismissed, the teacher spends time preparing for the upcoming unit. He prepares a list of words that most students will not know, developing a list for each week of the six-week period. Knowing words are defined differently in various dictionaries, he uses two dictionaries to record proper meanings for each word. Some things are not illustrated in the textbook so he decides it would be helpful to have pictures and he looks for illustrations in library resources. The textbook illustrates most procedures, but there is one process for which an illustration is not available. Knowing illustrations or flowcharts help students understand the process, the teacher decides to develop a transparency that illustrates the process. One aspect of the upcoming study involves events over time. The teacher considers having students develop a timeline in class, but he prefers to have it ready when the unit begins, so he prepares the timeline.

Always one to encourage outside reading, the teacher develops a list of library books and retrieves books and magazines to put on the "free time" reading shelf. The teacher wants to relate the unit to the real world and uses newspaper and magazine articles to establish this relationship. He must not forget the news databases because students will access those from computers in the classroom and the media center, so he spends time searching through periodicals and relevant databases.

He plans two or three hands-on activities for every unit and he does not want to use the same ones used last year. Needing to locate at least one new activity, he spends time browsing through project books and magazines to find an idea that fits the supplies and materials that are on hand. The textbook lists several reference sources with information pertinent to the text. The teacher wonders if these items are in the media center collection. Tempted to ask the media specialist to send any references that are available, he remembers her full schedule of information literacy activities and checks the media center catalog from his classroom computer. He wants someone from the community to speak to the class because students love to listen to people with first-hand information. He thinks about calling the public library, the local historical society, or the newspaper for a lead on a guest speaker, but time is running out. He must finish the current unit and begin the next. He thinks—maybe next year he will find a speaker.

What is wrong with this scenario? He is doing everything! He seems like a conscientious and well-prepared teacher, but his actions could be part of the reason the teacher feels so tired at the end of the school day. It is great for him to be up-to-date on the topic, but he is taking all the steps to be ready to spoon-feed the students. This is not the way to ensure students develop good information habits. In order to develop students who have ingrained habits of mind, the students should be taking the actions and making the decisions, with teacher oversight of course.

Eliot Eisner, an authority in effective schools, explains six things that really count in schools. Students need to learn: exploring ideas is fun and exciting, problem-solving strategies to use through life, to use various formats and sources, to stimulate their sense of wonder, they are part of a caring community, and to value their own unique importance (11). There is little doubt that when students acquire these habits of mind, they are doing things that really count.

# Sources Cited

American Association for the Advancement of Science. *Benchmarks for Science Literacy*. New York: Oxford University Press, 1993.

American Association for the Advancement of Science, Project 2061. *Science for All Americans*. Washington: AAAS, 1989 or <http://www.project2061.org/tools/sfaaol/chap12.htm>.

American Association of School Librarians. Association for Educational Communications and Technology. *Information Power: Building Partnerships for Learning*. Chicago: American Library Association, 1998.

Divesta, F. J., K. G. Hayward, and V. P. Orlando. "Developing Trends in Monitoring Text for Comprehension," *Child Development* 50 (1979): 97-105.

Eisenberg, Michael B., and Robert E. Berkowitz. *Curriculum Initiative: An Agenda and Strategy for Library Media Programs*. Norwood, NJ: Ablex 1990.

Eisner, E. W. "What Really Counts in Schools." *Educational Leadership* 48.3 (1991): 10-17.

"Habits of Mind." 28 June 2004 <http://web.csuchico.edu/~ah24/habits.htm>.

Kuhlthau, Carol. *Teaching the Library Research Process*. New York: Scarecrow Press, 1994.

Meier, Debbie. *The Power of Their Ideas*. 1995: (50-51) <http://www.essentialschools.org>.

Office of Educational Research and Improvement. "What Should Parents Know about Information Literacy?" Washington: Access Eric, 2000. unpaged. ED 460 787

## Source for Introductory Quote

Meier, Debbie. *The Power of Their Ideas*. 1995: 50-51 or <http://www.essentialschools.org>.

# 5

# Curriculum Implementation

> ... one of the major reasons why librarians are often overlooked by teachers is the lack of exposure during their teacher training programs to the types of value-added services librarians can provide.
>
> *- G. N. Hartzell*

When a library media specialist believes students will perform better in the classroom and on tests if they are information literate, the impetus for successful curriculum implementation exists. A media professional, backed by standards and a written curriculum, has the necessary tools to collaborate with other faculty members in teaching these skills. Teachers of academic disciplines now recognize how these skills help students learn more content. They are aware that information literate students:

- Understand how information is organized,
- Can interpret and organize it, and
- Are able to find information needed to fill-in gaps or for personal satisfaction.

Despite the growing awareness of the benefits students gain from having information skills, the library media specialist must sell an information literacy program and be prepared to do more than 50 percent of the work to get it underway. Once a program is established, experience shows that teachers value it and are willing to do their part.

# Looking Back at Skills Instruction

Library skills instruction, particularly for elementary and junior high schools, did not begin until the 1960s when federal funding provided staffing for those school libraries (Smith, *LMC Programs* 4). Until then, library instruction was offered mainly at high school libraries where instruction was provided for individuals or small groups who requested it. Instruction was given in response to a student's question or when an alert librarian noticed a student's perplexed look and offered help. No consideration was given to tying skill instruction to coursework, and coordination between the library and the teaching program was limited. Berner's groundbreaking book published in 1958 was the first to suggest an integrated approach, yet the profession was slow to adopt this approach.

School librarians tried numerous techniques and strategies to make library instruction effective. As each new media format became available, they tried it, but there were few successes, which led to overall discontent. Librarians at each school level thought those working with lower grades were not teaching library skills. College librarians believed all school librarians had failed to teach students how to locate and use materials. In large measure, this lack of success was because students were taught skills out of context. Library skills seemed unrelated to the courses that were important to students, those on which grades were given.

During the 1970s, the school library profession began giving serious study and thought about why their instructional efforts seemed so ineffective. Through study and experimentation, several important principles were discovered.

- Information skills are best learned in the context of coursework.
- A flexible schedule is more conducive to skill acquisition and application.
- Collaborative planning ensures skills are learned and applied.

Library media specialists believe these three principles are valid, but many teachers and administrators do not know or do not accept them.

There are several factors that have limited the success of putting these principles into practice. One factor is limited time, which is always an issue when trying to implement a new approach. Classroom schedules are packed and teachers think students do not have time to learn anything more. Limited contact with teachers is a second factor that works against successful integration of coursework and skill development. Hartzell underscores this problem in *Building Influence for the School Librarian*, yet he encourages librarians to participate in activities outside the library because "lacking engagement, other people simply are not aware of its value" (6). A third factor that works against integrated programs is the lack of information other educators have about media services. This lack of knowledge is understandable because training programs for teachers and administrators pay little or no attention to the media center and its place within the school program.

Despite the factors working against an integrated approach, the '80s saw many books and articles published to promote and explain it. The decade of the '90s saw real progress. Library media specialists were more successful in enlisting teacher cooperation to tie information skill instruction with course content. Cooperation rarely extended across an entire school, but at least there were pockets of real success. In large measure the new curricula and media standards provided the thought that stimulated action. The next section covers things a media specialist can do to promote an integrated, collaborative skill program.

# Understanding the Instructional Program

A media specialist needs to know what is taught in the instructional program and how it is taught. If the media specialist lacks this information, there can be little success in integrating information skill instruction into classroom content. There are four steps to take to know a school's program:

- Review courses of study included in the school curriculum.
- Review textbooks used for each subject.
- Review each teacher's lesson plans.
- Review media center resources related to the teaching plans.

Do not be alarmed thinking these reviews will take a lot of time. Each review is only cursory and will not require as much time as you might initially think. Whatever time it takes is worth it, because this knowledge gives a media specialist confidence when working with teachers. When possible, the course of study reviews and textbook reviews should be completed before the school year. Reviews of lesson plans and media center resources can be completed as the school year progresses. For example, review the lesson plans and resources for the upcoming grading period during the current period. These reviews equip the media specialist with the knowledge needed to show each teacher how her course content is tied to information skills.

## Review the Courses of Study

There should be a course-of-study or a curriculum document that provides an overview of every subject taught in the school. Often a copy of these documents is located in the library media center. If not, copies can usually be obtained from the principal's office, borrowed from the district's curriculum supervisor, or obtained online. Surveying these documents gives the media specialist a broad overview of instruction for each subject. Knowing the school's instructional program not only provides the background knowledge needed to communicate with teachers, but simultaneously provides information useful in collection development.

When the media specialist is prepared to discuss curriculum content, he is ready to initiate contact with the teachers and to seek their cooperation. Being aware of what teachers are trying to do demonstrates an interest and helps foster a "we're-in-this-together" mindset. Discussions with each teacher or teaching team should include examples that show how information skills relate to the content they teach. For example, knowing that a language arts teacher finds it difficult to teach students to recognize and develop metaphors, the media specialist might suggest using picture books that are easy to read and allow students to concentrate on any metaphors included. *Knots on a Counting Rope* is an example that might be shared with the teacher because this book uses the counting rope as a metaphor for passing time (qtd. in Hall 94).

### Review the Textbooks

Skim through each book or disk used to teach a course and make notes about the content, format, and special elements. Also notice the points that can be used to tie the course content to information literacy. Again, do not be overwhelmed by the prospect of this task for most textbooks can be technically reviewed in less than 20 minutes.

Table 5.1 outlines the process to use in reviewing a textbook (Smith, *Achieving* 35). Two examples follow the outline to illustrate the type of information gained through a technical review. The first example shows the results when a third grade, social studies textbook published by Harcourt was reviewed. The review took 15 minutes. The second review, a seventh grade book published by Glencoe Science, required 20 minutes.

Table 5.1

## Technical Review of a Textbook

As you review the text or disk, jot down notes about what you find.

**Step 1**
Read the title of the book and conjecture about its selection.

**Step 2**
See who wrote the book and if there is information about the author's qualifications.

**Step 3**
Survey the table of contents to note the coverage, arrangement, and special features of the book. Is the book in chronological order? Does it go from overview to detail or from detail to overview?

**Step 4**
Flip to the index at the back and skim to get a quick picture of the topics and people included in the book.

**Step 5**
Open the book to the first chapter to see how it is arranged. Are activities, tests, illustrations, or resource lists provided?

**Step 6**
Flip through the remaining chapters to see if there is a common arrangement, to notice illustrations, pictures, and ties to information literacy. Are there less topics covered but with more depth, or many topics covered with less depth? Does the content seem current?

**Step 7**
Is there a list of references used in writing the book? Are these references recently published? Are they available in the school collection?

# EXAMPLE #1

**Publisher:** Harcourt Brace
**Title:** Communities
**Series:** Harcourt Brace Social Studies

**Arrangement:**
> Six units, each begins with a literature selection and includes five to seven lessons.

**Contents:**
> What Is a Community?
> Where People Start Communities
> Communities Grow and Change
> People Working Together
> Living Together in a Community, State, and Nation
> The Many People of a Community

**References:**
> Glossaries, maps, biographical dictionary, timelines, gazetteer, index

**Study Aids:**
> New vocabulary highlighted, main idea stated, review questions, graphic organizers, unit projects

**Skills:**
> Reading maps, graphs, cutaway diagram and timelines, summarizing, using artifacts, interviewing

**Graphics:**
> Illustrations, land features, historical paintings, famous people, multicultural connections

# EXAMPLE #2

**Publisher:** Glencoe McGraw-Hill
**Title:** Alabama Science
**Series:** Glencoe Science

**Arrangement:**

Seven units, each unit has two to five chapters. Each chapter is correlated with state course of study objectives. Includes selections written by *Time* magazine staff and authors for the National Geographic Society. Teacher's edition available on CD-ROM.

**Contents:**

The Nature of Science
Life's Building Blocks and Processes
Reproduction and Heredity
Ecology
Earth and the Solar System
Building Blocks of Matter
Waves, Sound, and Light

**References:**

Safety symbols, periodic table of elements, index, glossaries, classes of organisms, map symbols, rock & mineral chart, math skills for science, field guide

**Study Aids:**

Study tips, vocabulary lists, questions, question study-folds

**Skills:**

Science Skill Handbook includes information organization (Venn Diagrams, concept mapping, network tree, events chain, cycle map, spider map), information analysis (compare & contrast, cause & effect, concluding, inferring,), and information sharing (database searching, spreadsheet development, computerized card catalog, graphics software, multimedia)

**Illustrations:**

Many small pictures, drawings, illustrated procedures, cutaway drawings

Note how many common concerns are evident in the social studies book to tie information literacy to social studies (map keys, globes, maps, charts, tables, and summarizing). This seventh-grade science textbook addresses database searching and graphic representations such as Venn diagrams. These common points provide avenues for teacher/media specialist collaboration.

## Review Lesson Plans

Some schools require every faculty member to file a copy of all lesson plans in the office or media center. This practice makes it easy for a media specialist to review teachers' instructional plans, but unfortunately this avenue is not always available. If a file of plans is not available, the media specialist can ask teachers to share their plans, explaining they are needed to help her become more informed about what students are learning in the classroom. Past experience has shown that many teachers will share, but some will not. Do not become discouraged if your requests are refused. There are other less direct ways to get the information. Two teachers teaching the same content in a school will generally use the same teaching pattern and materials, or students can tell you what the teacher is doing. Use the plans that can be obtained, and hope that a teacher who profits from sharing will pass along the message to the holdouts. Reviewing lesson plans reveals the instructional methods a teacher prefers, how she groups students, and the type of assessments employed.

## Review Media Center Resources

Automated catalogs have made the task of reviewing the collection to determine resources related to various areas of the instruction program much easier than it was because the computer does the searching that formerly had to be done by hand. The purpose of a collection review is to identify resources used in past semesters and to determine pertinent resources that are available but have not been used. Keyword searches using terms identified in the textbook's table of contents or index is a good way to locate related information available through the Internet or other locally-provided digital resources. It is particularly important to identify new materials related to classroom studies because students see these resources as the most attractive and desirable.

Once the media specialist is armed with the information needed to implement an information literacy curriculum, the next job is selling it to teachers and administrators. Sometimes this is difficult; sometimes it isn't. Situations can change from year to year. Media specialists who have worked in the same school for many years say teachers who cooperate and collaborate one year, may not the next. Changes occur because of faculty replacements or because a teacher's personal situation is different. When a district implements a new curriculum, teachers may be unwilling to undertake it and media center collaboration at the same time. Whatever the situation, a media specialist must continue to sell the information literacy program.

# Finding Implementation Opportunities

As the media specialist reviews curriculum materials, particularly textbooks and curriculum guides, she needs to make a chart of the areas to be studied during the year. Eisenberg and Berkowitz call this task curriculum mapping in their book *Curriculum Initiative* (71-85). While their term is apt, the map or chart is simply an overview of topics and skills taught in classrooms. This overview is important because it functions as a content calendar and reinforces the tie between coursework and information literacy skills. For example, when the media specialist sees "primary source report" on the ninth grade grid or "foreign country report" on the sixth grade grid, then she realizes research skills will be taught or reviewed.

There are many ties between coursework and information literacy. Vocabulary skills are integral to all courses. Figurative language is a tie in the study of poetry. Sequence of events, cause and effect, fact versus opinion, time and place, the use of maps, globes, and charts are common concerns with social studies. Math, being a symbol system, resembles organizational systems used in libraries. It also relates to information literacy through interpretation of graphic information.

Science and information literacy relate through classification of data, critical reading, summarizing, interpreting diagrams, and taking notes. The study of a foreign language provides an opportunity to relate a body of literature, to compare English and foreign words, and to become acquainted with the culture and life of the country. Music, like math, involves a symbol system that can be related to systems used in organizing and accessing information. Music terminology is also a fertile area for studying terms and word origins. Art provides avenues for interpretation and classification—two important areas in information literacy. There are so many common points with the study of English language arts that it is useless to begin comparing.

Any grade provides many ways to integrate information skills with content. Consider how the following list of eighth-grade topics are connected to information literacy skills:

English
- Elizabethan literature
- Implications of plagiarism
- Literary elements and devices

Science
- Reports on new scientific developments
- Evaluating the validity of a source
- Inferring from data

Social Studies
- Historical documents, Renaissance literature
- Biographies (Locke, Voltaire, Rousseau, Bolivar, Marx, Lenin, etc.)
- Maps and changing borders
- Comparing and contrasting times and places

Art
   • Lives of and influences on American artists

Math
   • Scale factor
   • Symbols

Special events also offer opportunities to connect information skills with classroom content. Events such as presidential elections, the Olympics, centennial celebrations, and various awards are things that interest and motivate students. At McCallie School, a prestigious school for boys in Chattanooga, the school librarian engages in many collaborative projects with teachers. Two eighth grade research projects are especially interesting. The first occurs every four years because it is a project that focuses on presidential primaries. Since this is the last presidential election before the eighth grade students will be old enough to vote, the project's purpose is to increase student knowledge of the election process and to heighten their awareness of current events and issues. Working in pairs, students develop a notebook on the candidate of their choice using online addresses provided by Jenny Salladay, the librarian. Resources they use include *NewsBank Middle School Edition* and *Middle School Plus*. Each completed notebook will contain background information that could be used to introduce the candidate at a political rally, to be a panelist on a TV talk show, to write a speech explaining how the candidate would help America, to develop a cartoon, a bumper sticker, or a political commercial.

In a second McCallie project, students role-play individuals involved in the Holocaust. Students can choose to be a victim, perpetrator, or a hero. Everyone, including Ms. Salladay and the teacher Dr. Ferrari, are charged with bringing to life the role they select and research. Resources and biographical tools purchased specially for this project include the *Encyclopedia of World Biography*, an excellent set of Holocaust biographies from Rosen Publishing, and *The Holocaust*, a four-volume set of encyclopedias by Grolier. Borrowing ideas from other practitioners may not be a new idea, but it continues to be a sound practice.

# Selling the Information Literacy Program

Armed with knowledge of the school program and equipped with implementation opportunities, a media specialist still must sell the information literacy program by showing how it contributes to student learning. Rarely will teachers knock on the library door asking the media specialist to help students become information literate; instead the library media specialist must convince the faculty about the relevance and importance of these skills. Perhaps the best approach is to think of it as a sales job and use four strategies to make the sale:

- Study the customers,
- Package the product by highlighting its most appealing points,
- Use a variety of marketing tools, and
- Employ good selling techniques.

Good techniques to use include having a clear message, highlighting the benefits, and keeping the costs reasonable. In this instance, costs are time and effort. Hartzell, in *Building Influence for the School Librarian*, suggests the following tactics to enlist faculty participation:

- Offer technology expertise and access as bribes to the collaboration,
- Work on committees to promote collegiality, and
- Undertake teacher recognition projects (154-164).

Debra Kay Logan says her experience suggests gathering statistics and using them to broadcast success. "As I was building my program, teachers often thanked me for working with them. When they did, I asked them to share their experience with others. 'Word of mouth' is truly the best advertising!" (3). Vary the publicity approach as needed but keep the goal in sight. The goal is to collaborate with every teacher to ensure all students become information literate and use library resources routinely in their classroom studies.

# Collaborating Is the Best Implementation Method

Collaboration is the best implementation approach. Cooperation is the next best approach, and going it alone is the least productive, but any of the three approaches can result in information literate students. It is far more difficult when a media specialist has to go it alone because the reality and importance of course content is missing.

It is likely a media specialist will be engaged in all three planning approaches in most schools because the willingness of teachers will vary from class to class and from year to year.

There are some situations where the ground for collaboration or cooperation is simply not fertile and there are schools where opportunities are bountiful. In schools where few faculty members can be convinced to collaborate, the media specialist must plan skill instruction alone and wait for new opportunities to sell reluctant faculty.

The point made time after time in this book is that the best way for students to learn information literacy skills is to learn and practic them in conjunction with course content. In this approach, the teacher or teaching team and the media specialist jointly plan a unit of instruction that engages students in finding and using information related to the topic being studied. Correlation with course content is important because students are motivated to learn these skills when they see real-life application—and a student's real-life revolves around the classroom. Betty Buckingham, a former Iowa state consultant for school libraries, once said that teaching library skills in isolation was like trying to teach a boy to swim without water. She compared it to showing a boy how to move his arms and legs while sprawled on a tabletop and then reminding him to do the same thing when he gets in the water! Students who learn information literacy skills in relation to course content are less likely to drown in the sea of information.

An old adage is that two heads are better than one. This rule applies to collaborative planning because it combines the expertise of two professionals. The teacher is the content specialist and the library media specialist is the information specialist. Students benefit when the two professionals combine their efforts. For example, students who learn textual organization principles are better able to navigate a textbook. Students who know how to organize can better prepare class papers and presentations. Each professional's role is unique, but both have a common interest in student achievement. Stavley suggests "the best way to characterize the allocation of responsibilities among teachers and librarians is to assign the task of fostering curiosity to teachers and the task of nourishing it to librarians" (4).

Although library media professionals are fervent as revival preachers about the saving graces of a collaborative approach, not everyone gets the message. The practice is still limited despite reams of written material and hundreds of presentations encouraging it. There are many reasons why collaboration is found more often in print than in practice. First, it requires teachers to change their working patterns and to see the school librarian as a contributing and equal teaching partner. This is not the picture many teachers have of media specialists, despite the fact that most states require a person to have a teaching certificate before they can be eligible for library media certification.

Lack of time is a second barrier. Planning takes time, although it requires less and less time as collaborators work together. Some teachers feel overwhelmed, under pressure, and are reluctant to try something new. The third and most unfortunate barrier to collaboration is the reluctance of some library media specialists to participate because they feel unprepared, uncertain, or indifferent. Toni Buzzeo gives other reasons why collaboration is limited, particularly in elementary schools.

- Increased insistence on uninterrupted blocks of time for reading and math instruction.
- Non-collaborative school cultures.
- Unsupportive school administrators.
- Inadequate library staffing that results in overtaxed media specialists.
- Outdated perceptions of the role of the librarian.
- Rigid library schedules (34).

Despite the barriers, library media specialists continue selling collaborative planning because they know everyone profits. Selling collaborative planning to a teacher is similar to a student attending his first middle school dance. Entering the dance hall, he must first scan the room for a partner, despite being aware others are watching to see how well he dances. Next he asks a partner to dance using favorable language and with a sincere smile. The third stage is getting in the groove, and the last stage is reflecting on the performance. In summary, a media specialist must make an interesting offer, keep in step, and evaluate what needs to change.

Successful collaboration needs administrative support because planning requires time during the regular school schedule, and collaborative activities do not always fit within the school structure. It flourishes when there is a team spirit among the faculty because feelings of shared respect allow each individual to try something new and to falter or fail without fear of ridicule or rejection. Successful collaboration requires more intense personal interaction and adequate methods of communication. E-mail has made it easier to collaborate.

Collaboration requires each professional to work toward a common goal even though their roles are different. Openness and collegiality are so important it is one for all and all for one. Most importantly, success requires having a vision and believing that students will achieve more when we work together. The five keys for successful collaboration are administrative support, mutual appreciation, avenues for sustained communication, a common language, and a shared vision.

There are many benefits from collaborating. Thomas mentions the opportunity for students to interact with two professionals instead of one (18). Having two teachers instead of one increases the likelihood a student will receive individual attention when it is needed. There are also occasions when the personalities of a student and a teacher collide. At these times, there is a second person who can step in to help analyze the problem and seek a solution. Collaboration also provides opportunities for the media specialist and teacher to share ideas, to discuss progress, and to learn from each other. Teachers will learn more about information handling and resources while the media specialist will learn more about classroom content. Both professionals gain teaching expertise through planning, implementing, evaluating, and reflecting on the students' performance.

## Notes on Collaboration

Do not worry about making a perfect plan when you collaborate. Often a teacher and media specialist work on a plan until it is refined enough to be published! That approach takes too long and having such a high standard when planning tends to limit and discourage it. A plan is simply a means of joint thinking and communicating. It is sharing ideas and strengthening a professional relationship that are the true benefits of collaborating. Any plan should only be used once and then the plan needs to be reviewed, revised, or discarded.

The plans you have made and implemented can provide useful lessons for other media specialists. Look for opportunities to share your experiences with others and to gain ideas and information from them. This type of sharing also presents an opportunity to improve the evaluation measures being used. Other professionals may have developed measures such as response sheets, rubrics, or checklists that they are willing to share. Collaboration is not just a process for teachers and media specialists to use; it works well when library media specialists try it.

Be patient when trying to implement collaborative planning. "People need 20 to 30 trials with any new procedure before they achieve comfort and control" (Joyce et al. 36). In the beginning, participants in collaborative planning are bound to be anxious because it is not customary to work or plan together. Just do the best you can and realize that with experience the process becomes easier and easier.

## *Checklist for Collaboration*
- Planning is an ongoing activity through the year.
- The school administration endorses collaborative planning.
- A written lesson plan designates activities and responsibilities.
- Both professionals are responsible for planning, preparation, and instruction.
- Both professionals monitor progress in implementing the plan.
- Both professionals are responsible for assessment.
- Both professionals are responsible for group management.
- Both professionals reflect on the outcomes of the lesson.
- There is an avenue for either professional to address concerns or frustrations.
- There is a way to revise the lesson plan if needed by either professional.
- Library resources augment and enrich classroom materials.
- Students learn information skills.
- Students learn content and subject-related skills.
- Students are engaged in information retrieval as individuals and small groups.
- There is mutual regard for the collaborative partner.
- There is a shared vision about outcomes.

# Sources Cited

Berner, Eliza. *Integrating Library Instruction with Classroom Teaching at Plainview Junior High.* Chicago: ALA, 1958.

Buzzeo, Toni. "Disciples of Collaboration." *School Library Journal* 48.9 (2002): 34.

Donham, Jean, Kay Bishop, Carol Collier Kuhlthau, and Dianne Oberg. *Inquiry-Based Learning: Lessons from Library Power.* Worthington, OH: Linworth Publishing, 2001.

Eisenberg, Michael B., and Robert E. Berkowitz. *Resource Companion for Curriculum Initiative: An Agenda and Strategy for Library Media Programs.* Norwood, NJ: Ablex Publishing, 1988.

Grover, Robert. "Collaboration." [Lessons Learned Series] Sponsored by the American Association of School Librarians. (1996) Chicago: American Library Association.

Hall, Susan. *Using Picture Storybooks to Teach Literary Devices: Recommended Books for Children and Young Adults.* Phoenix: Oryx Press, 1990.

Hartzell, Gary N. *Building Influence for the School Librarian.* [The Professional Growth Series] Worthington, OH: Linworth Publishing, 1994.

Joyce, Bruce, J. Wolf, and E. Calhoun. *The Self-Renewing School.* Alexandria, VA: ACSD, 1993.

Logan, Debra Kay. *Information Skills Toolkit: Collaborative Integrated Instruction for the Middle Grades.* Worthington, OH: Linworth Publishing, 2000: 3.

Medley, Kelly Payne. "Would You Like to Collaborate?" *Library Talk* 15.1 (2002): 16.

Smith, Jane Bandy. *Achieving a Curriculum-Based Library Media Center Program: The Middle School Model for Change.* Chicago: American Library Association, 1995: 56.

---. *Library Media Center Programs for Middle Schools: A Curriculum-Based Approach.* Chicago: American Library Association, 1989.

Stavley, Tony. "Hunting and Gathering in an Information Explosion." <http://web.keene.edu/~tstavely/edozarticles/21stcentlib.html>.

Thomas, Melody. "What Is Collaboration to You? *Library Talk* 15.2 (2002): 17.

## Source for Introductory Quote

Hartzell, G.N. "The Invisible School Librarian: Why Other Educators Are Blind to Your Value." *School Library Journal* 43.11 (1997): 24-29.

# 6

# Effective Teaching

> You must never tell a thing. You must illustrate it. We learn through the eye and not the noggin.
>
> *- Will Rogers*

Turns out that Professor Higgins knew a thing or two about effective teaching when he wanted to turn flower girl Eliza Doolittle into a lady. He had clear purpose, stayed on task, illustrated proper behavior, gave her opportunities to practice, and provided prompt feedback to correct any errors. Most importantly, he believed she would be successful. Teachers and media specialists could take lessons from Professor Higgins.

We know more about effective teaching today because good teachers have shared their experiences, researchers have reported on strategies that work, and cognitive psychologists have discovered more about how people learn. Before 1960, few studies focused on the elements of effective teaching. However, in the mid-'60s, Coleman and his colleagues ignited a controversy with their report to the U.S. Congress on effects of segregated schools. The result was dissolution of neighborhood schools and initiation of busing (Britannica Online). In the wake of these changes, many school-effects studies were initiated in an effort to find out what really did matter in schooling. As a result, the decade of the 80s was characterized as an "extraordinary time in the history of research on teaching" (Wittrock 214). This chapter capsules what we learned about the elements of good instruction.

# Library Media Specialists as Teachers

Many may wonder why a book for library media specialists includes a chapter on effective teaching. There are several reasons. First, a media specialist is a teacher, so she must know how a successful teacher behaves. Secondly, a media specialist works with classroom teachers and knowing the elements of good teaching prepares a media specialist to help diagnose problems and suggest resources to address those needs.

Many classroom teachers do not see school media professionals as teachers. They still view the library as a depository for materials and the school librarian as a custodian instead of an instructional partner. If the media program is to achieve its potential, this viewpoint must change. The person best positioned to bring about the needed change is the library media specialist. Armed with knowledge about good teaching and the school's curriculum, the media specialist can demonstrate how the media center and the classroom can be tied together through the common thread of course information and information skills.

Media specialists know how course content relates to information literacy, but many teachers are blind to the connection. This situation must be corrected before course content can be the driving force for information skill instruction. Information is the basis for every course, which means information literacy is integral to every subject. There are differences in the degree of relationship because skill-based subjects, such as mathematics, physical education, and foreign languages are less related than content-rich courses, such as social studies and science, but all coursework requires information handling.

A media specialist must illustrate how courses and information skills relate before she can recruit teachers to participate in collaborative planning. This task requires having specific examples on hand rather than speaking in generalities; yet experience shows that once a teacher reaps the advantages of collaboration, he will be a convert. Collaboration begins when the media specialist communicates with a teacher.

Communication is facilitated when the media specialist knows what each teacher believes about how classrooms should operate. Any teacher's philosophy has been influenced by an amalgamation of personal psychology, experiences, and training. While a teacher might not be able to vocalize her teaching philosophy, a media specialist who is aware of various teaching philosophies can determine a teacher's beliefs by observing in the classroom and posing pertinent questions. For example, contrasting two teaching philosophies, behaviorism and constructivism, makes it easy to see how classroom philosophy can differ.

# Two Teaching Philosophies

Teachers usually teach the way they were taught—usually, but not always. Older faculty members may differ from younger ones because training programs and attitudes change over time. A personal experience illustrates this point. Thirty years ago, the elementary school librarian introduced board games as part of the library's collection. These games were available for library use before and after school or for students to play during the day with the teacher's permission. Younger teachers saw availability of board games as an opportunity for students to learn through play, a way for them to reward good performance, and a service that made the library seem a more "with-it" place. The older teachers, however, complained to the principal that the librarian was encouraging students to waste time and sending the wrong message from the library.

Age is not the only factor that causes teachers to have different opinions about teaching and learning. A teacher's belief system has even greater influence. One teacher believes drill and practice is a good way to teach, while another teacher thinks repetitive practice is a boring waste of time. One teacher believes young students learn through structured play while another thinks games are only for the playground or gym. One teacher thinks multimedia is a stimulating teaching method while another feels a loss of control because media dictates the message. Students in one classroom work quietly at their desks while the next room sounds like a beehive as students work in groups at tables. It is important for a library media specialist to recognize and value the unique characteristics of teachers because their philosophies, like their personalities, are internalized. A media specialist should try to accommodate each teacher's style and preference.

## *Behaviorism*

Teachers who are behaviorists see students as sponges. Students will soak up knowledge if it is poured on. This philosophy is based on belief in the stimulus-response theory fostered by behavioral psychologists Thorndike and Skinner. It is predicated on the way animals responded in laboratory tests. A behaviorist teacher provides a stimulus to elicit student response and learning is measured by each student's response. When one step is accomplished the next step is introduced. According to this philosophy, curriculum should be broken into small components and taught in a hierarchical sequence (Rowan 117).

Mastery Learning is one interpretation of behaviorism. It is an instruction method formulated in the early 1970s by John B. Caroll and Benjamin Bloom (Joyce, Weil, and Calhoun 323). Caroll believed students could learn any material given appropriate structure and time on task. To target instruction, the curriculum was organized into small blocks so each student worked at the appropriate stage. The curriculum was often packaged in study units so students in the same classroom could work at different levels. The central tenet was that a student had to master one step before beginning the next. When a student failed, the content had to be taught again using alternative strategies and materials.

Direct instruction also grew out of behavioral psychology. It is similar to mastery learning because it involves highly sequenced and structured teaching; however full class instruction is more common than individualized instruction. An essential aspect of direct instruction is diagnosing each learner to determine prerequisite knowledge or skills. Remediation is provided for learners who are not ready for class instruction. The work by Joyce, Weil, and Calhoun explains the five phases of direct instruction.

Phase one is orientation where the teacher prepares students for the unit by motivating them and explaining how the material connects what they already know. Presentation is phase two and it takes many forms to provide students with a lesson's content. The last three phases involve practice: structured practice has students following as the teacher models the desired performance, in guided practice, has each student acting alone although carefully observed by the teacher; independent practice encourages variation, innovation, and competence.

In behaviorist classrooms, tests are frequent and usually require short answers. Students must show competence at one level before they can move to the next. Test items usually have one right answer, most often the one found in the textbook. Some educators dislike these types of tests because students are required to do little more than regurgitate answers from the text or lecture.

Many teachers like mastery learning and direct instruction because of the structure inherent in both curriculum and classroom management. Inexperienced teachers often find support in these methods because they are structured and the teacher is in control. Yet, critics of this approach complain it can damage students' self-concept and confidence if they fail to reach mastery and that it limits creativity and initiative.

## Constructivism

Individuals who embrace a constructivist philosophy believe learning occurs when an individual connects new information with existing information. This view of learning sees each individual as having a unique set of experiences and influences. Instruction must respond to each student's needs and interests so classroom instruction cannot be carefully scripted as it is in mastery learning.

Constructivism emerged from cognitive research. These studies revealed that learning frequently occurs without the information being structured from simple to complex. Often individuals who were given the same information learned different parts of it due to prior knowledge, while some individuals did not learn any of it. They also discovered that students could learn something considered too mature or complex if they could relate it to something already known.

In a constructivist classroom, a teacher guides, clarifies, responds, and encourages instead of directing because the classroom is student-centered instead of teacher-centered. Loertscher distinguishes these as a teacher being "guide on the side" versus a "sage on the stage" (73-74). The focus is on students learning big ideas rather than narrowly prescribed content (Fosnot 29-30). A constructivist teacher may challenge students with a problem, preferably one set in a realistic context—where actual data and primary sources provide the information they need to devise a solution. Students use higher-order thinking to solve the problem because they question, challenge, and defend their ideas. Teachers model higher order thinking, revealing to students how difficult it is to think through a problem. "By focusing on puzzlements and contradictions, the teacher establishes the notion that ideas are complicated and worthy of time … and that each student is capable of formulating interesting ideas" (Julyan and Duckworth 71). Students assume responsibility for their own learning because much of what they learn is personal and unique. They learn, in part, by analyzing their errors.

Testing in a constructivist classroom is more complex than in a behaviorist classroom because it is concerned as much with process as it is with content. Tests are designed to challenge students, to make them elaborate, and to call forth diverse ideas. The focus of construction on big ideas means that tests measure knowledge of concepts and principles instead of facts and figures. Test items may have more than one right answer or there may not be a clear, correct answer.

Proponents support constructivism because it promotes exploration, encourages higher-order thinking, fosters student independence, stimulates creativity, and values alternative ideas or opinions. Those who want to know more about constructivist philosophy should locate a copy of *Inquiry-Based Learning*, a recent publication that explains how the Library Power project encouraged implementation of the constructivist philosophy through the inquiry approach (Donham et al.). Inquiry is a technique preferred by constructivist teachers because instead of telling students what they need to know, the teacher proposes a task, problem, or question for students to analyze and answer. In the Donham book, Kuhlthau endorses the inquiry approach because it allows a teacher to "... build on what children know, provide different ways of learning, and offer opportunities for social interaction to develop higher-order thinking and understanding." Constructivism promotes:

- Active engagement,
- Building on prior knowledge,
- Developing higher-order thinking,
- Supporting developmental stages and different ways of learning, and
- Considering social interaction as an instrument of construction (10-11).

Students can learn in classrooms whether constructivist or behaviorist, although each approach requires different strategies and techniques. An example illustrates how different strategies achieve the same objectives. Suppose the instructional objectives are for students to be able to recognize properties of physical matter and to describe how these properties can change.

In a behaviorist classroom, students would be asked to use the textbook to specify different physical properties (mass, hardness, viscosity, fluidity, color, taste, and conductivity), and then to identify two examples of each. Once a test showed most of the students could identify the properties and give an example for each, the class would investigate how each property could change. Students who failed to grasp the concept would use similar, but different, activities to reach the objectives.

In a constructivist classroom, the teacher might conduct an experiment that demonstrated a change in properties and ask the students to explain what happened. As students raised questions and discussed the results of the experiment, one student would make class notes on a transparency. After the class grouped their questions and concerns into areas of study, individuals or small groups would select an area and embark on further investigation, or vary the experiment to further test the results. The teacher would monitor the activities in case an adjustment or some clarification was needed to keep students on track to accomplish the two objectives. Later the class will come together for students to share what they learned. Their comments will guide the teacher in developing a classroom test on changing properties.

# Teaching Methods

Just as faculty members embrace different teaching philosophies, they may also prefer different teaching methods and techniques. In this chapter, the term "method" means an overall process, such as the Socratic method involves asking structured questions as a means of leading students to knowledge. A "technique" is a means of presenting material, providing practice, or assessing student learning. A variety of techniques can be used with any method. Table 6.1 illustrates how various instructional techniques can be used with six methods.

Table 6.1

## Teaching Methods and Instructional Techniques

| Methods | Instructional Techniques | | | | | | | |
|---|---|---|---|---|---|---|---|---|
| Socratic | Question | Pose situations | | | | | | |
| Didactic | Tell | Explain | Elaborate | Lecture | Describe | Interpret | Summarize | |
| Demonstrate | Use | Select | Write | Make | Show | Construct | Draw | Create |
| Simulate | Pretend | Participate | | | | | | |
| Investigate | Analyze | Identify | Distinguish | Locate | | | | |
| Associate | Compare | Contrast | Infer | Predict | Relate | Discuss | | |

Methods and techniques should vary in response to the students and course situations, yet there are pros and cons for every method and technique. Lecture is effective for teaching fundamentals of a course. It is an efficient way to provide information that would take much longer for students to find on their own. Discussion involves students in considering a question or problem from various viewpoints. While this approach encourages students to share opinions and stimulates student thinking, the discussion can get off-track. In a deductive teaching method, the topic or skill is first presented as a whole and then dissected into parts. This is a time-efficient way to convey information, and the dissection provides a framework for learning, however the teacher dominates instruction and the students remain passive. Inductive teaching is the reverse of deductive teaching because it moves from parts to a whole. Some students have difficulty assembling the pieces into a whole, instead they get lost amid the pieces. Inquiry is a method that takes time and requires student involvement. Students can move from observation to generalization although they need many related experiences to be able to grasp a concept (Burden and Byrd 82-83). This approach demands a teacher who is creative and flexible; many people would say the characteristics of a good teacher.

# Characteristics of Good Teachers

Everyone seems to have an opinion about what makes a good teacher. Some people believe teaching is an art and effective practitioners are born with the skill. Other people believe it is a science and can be learned like anything else. Highet comes down on the side of art. On the back cover of his book about teaching, he wrote "Teaching is not like inducing a chemical reaction: it is much more like painting a picture or making a piece of music." Madeline Hunter took the side of science when she wrote "Teaching is one of the last professions to emerge from the stage of 'witch doctoring' and become a profession based on a science of learning (169)." The question of whether teaching is an art or a science, or a little of both remains unanswered, but there is growing agreement about the characteristics of good teachers.

A good teacher establishes contact with students and encourages them to cooperate with one another. According to a survey conducted by the American Association of Higher Education (qtd. in Hitch 23), good teachers engage students in active learning, give prompt feedback, assure students spend time-on-task, expect success, and respect diverse talents and ways of learning. Hart surveyed high school seniors and found they preferred teachers with a sense of humor and those who gave clear directions and used examples in teaching. They disliked teachers who were aloof, sarcastic, or grouchy (qtd. in Hamachek 341). In a review of teacher effectiveness studies, he found teachers were preferred who

- Have a sense of humor,
- Are fair and democratic,
- Vary their level of interaction with students,
- Use outside resources,
- Are flexible,
- See the student's point of view,
- Are willing to try new things,
- Are knowledgeable,
- Are skillful questioners, and
- Use a conversational tone in teaching (35-36).

Glenn believes a good teacher maximizes learning time by making smooth transitions from one activity to the next. In comparison, ineffective teachers waste class time because of inefficient routines for distributing papers, assigning homework, and other class routines. Other qualities Glenn found effective teachers have are enthusiasm and an ability to communicate clearly and question effectively. Most importantly, they have high expectations for all students (19-20). To summarize, then, traits of an effective teacher encompass personality, techniques, and abilities.

# Keys to Effective Teaching

After surveying professional literature, eight keys to effective teaching were chosen by the author and are briefly addressed in the following section. Factors mentioned most often as keys to successful teaching are

- Expect all students to achieve,
- Be enthusiastic,
- Make the purpose of the lesson clear,
- Model desired behavior,
- Vary the pace of instruction,
- Vary the techniques, strategies, and resources used,
- Ask good questions and give appropriate wait time, and
- Reflect on student performance.

The following sections briefly highlight each of the eight keys to effective teaching.

### Expect All Students to Achieve

An individual tends to perform as expected. Rosenthal and Jacobson in *Pygmalion in the Classroom* illustrate the impact of a self-fulfilling prophecy that occurs when a teacher believes certain students will achieve, or conversely, believes they will not succeed. In their study, teachers were told certain students were "ready to bloom" intellectually and the teachers should expect a burst of achievement, even though the students had been chosen at random. By the end of the year, the children identified as "ready to blossom" really did show greater gains (91). These students achieved, in large measure, because the teachers expected them to achieve.

"To summarize our speculations, we may say that by what she said, by how and when she said it, by her facial expressions, postures, and perhaps by her touch, the teacher may have communicated to the children of the experimental group that she expected improved intellectual performance" (180).

In a research review on teacher expectations, Thomas L. Good cites studies that show how a teacher's behavior changes when working with students thought to be low performers. Teachers were more likely to:

- Demand less performance,
- Give less sincere praise,
- Interrupt student speech,
- Offer fewer opportunities to respond,
- Reduce wait time,
- Give more criticism,
- Make less eye contact,
- Give fewer smiles, and
- Make less use of student ideas (34).

Unfortunately, many of the factors that cause teachers to react negatively to students are factors over which students have no control: race, physical unattractiveness, socioeconomic status, and native language. Whatever the cause, even young children are quickly alerted to a teacher's negative perception. Babad and associates found it took only ten seconds for even very young students to detect whether the teacher interacted with and liked a student (qtd. in Kauchak and Eggen 119). In this book, Kauchak and Eggen advise instructors to:

- Call on all students in equal measure,
- Give feedback to all students and equally to both sexes,
- Prompt the student for an acceptable answer when asking questions,
- Make eye contact with all students, and
- Change the seating arrangement regularly to allow all students to sit at the front of the room (120).

### Be Enthusiastic

An enthusiastic teacher is a motivating force. Learners are energized when a teacher varies his voice level, uses gestures, and moves around the room. However, teacher enthusiasm does not mean giving pep talks or staging theatrics; instead it means for teachers to express a genuine interest in the subject or topic being taught (Good and Brophy 368). Although some studies suggest the effect of a teacher's enthusiasm on student response, it just makes sense that an enthusiastic presenter creates interest in a topic. If the presenter or organizer of an event is lethargic, those attending become distracted and disinterested.

### Make the Purpose of the Lesson Clear

It is easier to achieve when a person knows the intent of a lesson. Clearly explain what students are expected to do. Most resources on good teaching mention the importance of establishing clear instructional intent, and a related point is to be certain students understand your directions. Do not repeat them unnecessarily, but ask for enough feedback to gauge student understanding.

### Model Desired Behavior

Modeling is defined as "the display of behaviors that are imitated by others" (Kauchak and Eggen 117). Modeling can be an effective way to teach, particularly when students are learning a skill. For example, teach students how to summarize a passage by thinking aloud so students can follow the mental process used to identify the key elements, arrange them in logical fashion, and connect the elements in a written paragraph or sentence. Many testify about the impact of a good model on student learning and classroom behavior. When students see their teachers read, study, and grapple with new ideas, they apply those behaviors to their own work. A good model is honest. Someone who says one thing and does another is not a good classroom model because students are more likely to do what you do than what you say.

### Vary the Pace of Instruction

Students learn best when a lesson is well timed. When the flow of information is too slow, students become bored and inattentive. If the flow is too fast, they become lost and disengaged, or become discipline problems. The importance of pacing not only refers to the flow of information, but also to classroom management. A teacher needs to have good time management skills when conducting a lesson. A good manager will not dwell too long on directions and will distribute papers and accomplish similar routine tasks in a timely, efficient manner. He will move smoothly from one activity to another without interruption, knowing that students will not maintain focus if they are waiting for directions or materials. Good teachers arrange the classroom in a manner that allows efficient movement, which facilitates smooth transition. In chapter five of their book, Good and Brophy suggest eight issues for good pacing:

- Know your own teaching tempo.
- Watch for cues that students are getting bored.
- Provide short breaks for lessons that last longer than 30 minutes.
- Use discussion or review to break-up activities.
- Vary instructional strategies.
- Avoid interrupting the flow of the lesson by dwelling too long on one portion.
- Summarize at the end of each lesson segment.

## *Vary the Techniques, Strategies, and Resources Used*

Goodlad's landmark book, *A Place Called School*, laments the lack of variation found in schools. This experienced educator found that 90 percent of all classroom instruction was passive and focused on teaching facts and isolated concepts instead of big ideas (86). He paints a picture of staid and rigid instruction, and it is disappointing to learn about the sameness of instruction when we know that variety helps keep students interested and engaged.

Even teachers who strive for variety can fall into a routine that results in using the same materials and techniques repeatedly. To avoid this instruction flaw, it is wise to review instructional plans from time to time with an eye for variety. Library media specialists can help teachers add variety to their instruction by suggesting resources that are new to the collection, or items that have not been used in the past, or information drawn from the Internet. Media and materials are the easiest way to vary instruction, but they must be used because they add to the lesson, not just used to take up time. Choose media only after considering characteristics of the learners, the teaching strategy, the subject matter, and other instructional activities.

Heinich, Molenda, and Russell guide teachers in using the media instruction through the ASSURE model. This model prompts teachers to analyze learners, state objectives, select media materials, utilize materials, require learner performance, and evaluate/revise (qtd. in Burden and Byrd 133). One of the most important principles related to media use is for instructors to review the materials and know the content. A teacher should ensure the facility is conducive to using the media and the format should be selected because it best fits the lesson not because it is easier to use.

Media can be a powerful facet of teaching because it motivates, is time-efficient, and standardizes instruction. Library media specialists believe in the power of media but they know that its usefulness depends upon it being integrated with instruction. Most media specialists have experienced a teacher who comes running into the media center in search of a video or DVD. Asked what it needs to be about, the teacher responds, "about thirty minutes." Obviously, using media in this way will not result in effective instruction. Yet media can be an effective means of teaching students because it is the closest substitute for the actual experience.

## Ask Good Questions and Give Appropriate Wait Time

Research on effective questioning has been approached from different perspectives:

- Calling for responses,
- Types of questions,
- Responding to responses, and
- Waiting for responses.

When calling for a response to a question, is it better to call on students at random or to use a structured approach? When a random pattern is used, students are more engaged because a question may be directed at any one of them. When a structured pattern is used such as alphabetical order or going down a row, students may disengage except when their turn is approaching.

What type of questions should be asked? There are questions that focus attention, questions that prompt more questions, and there are questions that probe how much a student knows. Focusing questions call attention to the lesson and these questions can be used to motivate or evaluate. Prompting questions can help students answer an earlier question or can help a student analyze an incorrect response. Probing questions force a student to clarify or analyze his initial response (Moore 178-184). Teachers or media specialists who improvise questions on the spur of the moment are likely to ask many irrelevant, confusing, and poor questions. Good questions help structure the lesson, are appropriate to the level of the students, are asked in a logical sequence, and vary in their purpose.

What is the best way for a teacher to respond to a student's answer? According to Feldman, "teachers use some form of turn-taking, either random or ordered" (8). Calling on students at random causes everyone to stay alert, but some students may be overlooked. An ordered selection pattern makes certain everyone is asked to answer a question, but after answering a question a student may disengage. Combining both approaches seems best. Responding to student answers is also important because these are opportunities to provide feedback to students. At these times a teacher has an opportunity to compliment a student, unravel confusion, or correct misinformation.

Wait time is an issue related to questioning that has been studied by many researchers. This term means the amount of time a teacher waits for a student to give an answer. The average wait time is only a second or two, which is too little time for students to think about the question. Burden & Byrd found a longer wait time not only allowed students to think about the question, but it also provided opportunities for students to talk with each other about the question and to think it through more carefully (112). Similarly, Rowe discovered that extending wait time as much as two seconds resulted in better student responses.

### *Reflect on Student Performance*

Kottkamp explains reflection as meaning the process of "paying deliberate, analytical attention" (182). Reflection requires stepping back and trying to see the teaching and learning experience from an objective view. It is a valuable process for both teachers and students. Dewey was one of the first educators to dwell on the importance of students thinking about what they had learned as a means of learning more. That was John Dewey, not Melvin! Writing is an effective way to describe, dissect, and discuss what happened in class. A writing reflection may be a journal, case record, metaphor, or a critical incident report. When reflecting on a lesson, use the effective teaching checklist to guide your evaluation.

# Checklist for Effective Teaching

- Give clear directions and check to see if they are understood.

- Explain the purpose of the lesson and relate it to what students know.

- Give opportunities for students to ask questions.

- Show respect for the questions students ask.

- Explain things simply and give illustrative examples.

- Give students time to think.

- Teach at a pace appropriate to the age and abilities of the students.

- Give students many opportunities to practice.

- Give prompt feedback so students correct errors and gain confidence.

- Review frequently to see if the content has been learned.

# Sources Cited

*Britannica Online*. "Coleman, James S." 10 Mar. 2004 <http://search.ed.com/article?eu=691&tocid=0&query=coleman%20study%20on%20schoo…>.

Burden, Paul R., and David M. Byrd. *Methods for Effective Teaching*. Boston: Allyn, 1994.

Donham, Jean, Kay Bishop, Carol Collier Kuhlthau, and Dianne Oberg. *Inquiry-Based Learning: Lessons from Library Power*. Worthington, OH: Linworth, 2001.

Feldman, Sandra. "The Right Line of Questioning." *Teaching PreK-8* 33.4 (2003): 8.

Fosnot, Catherine T. *Constructivism: Theory, Perspectives, and Practice*. New York: Teachers College P., 1996.

Glenn, Robert E. "What Teachers Need to Be." *Education Digest* 67.1 (2001): 19-21.

Good, Thomas L. "Two Decades of Research on Teacher Expectations: Findings and Future Directions." *Journal of Teacher Education* 35 (1987): 32-47.

Good, Thomas L., and Jere E. Brophy. *Looking in Classrooms*. 7th ed. New York: Longman, 1997.

Goodlad, John I. *A Place Called School: Prospects for the Future*. New York: McGraw, 1983.

Hamachek, Don. "Characteristics of Good Teachers and Implications for Teacher Education." *Teaching Today: Tasks and Challenges*. Ed. J. Michael Palardy. New York: Macmillan, 1975. 33-42.

Heinich, R., Molenda, M., Russell, J.D., and Smaldino, S.E. *Instructional Media and Technologies for Learning*. 7th ed. Upper Saddle River, NJ: Pearson Educational, 2002.

Highet, Gilbert. *The Art of Teaching*. New York: Vintage, 1989.

Hitch, Leslie P. "Aren't We Judging Virtual University by Outdated Standards?" *Journal of Academic Librarianship* 26.1 (2000): 21-27.

Hunter, Madeline. "Knowing, Teaching and Supervising." *Using What We Know about Teaching*. Ed. P. L. Hosford. Alexandria, VA: ASCD, 1984. 169-192.

Joyce, Bruce, Marsha Weil, and Emily Calhoun. *Models of Teaching*. 6th ed. Boston: Allyn and Bacon, 1999.

Julyan, C., and E. Duckworth. "A Constructivist Perspective on Teaching and Learning Science." *Constructivism: Theory, Perspectives, and Practice.* Ed. C. T. Fosnot. New York: Teachers College P., 1996. 55-72.

Kauchak, Donald P., and Paul D. Eggen. *Learning and Teaching: Research-Based Methods.* Boston: Allyn, 1998.

Kottkamp, Robert B. "Means for Facilitating Reflection." *Education & Urban Society* 22.2 (1990): 182-204.

Loertscher, David V. *Taxonomies of the School Library Media Program.* 2nd ed. San Jose, CA: Hi Willow, 2000.

Moore, Kenneth D. *Classroom Teaching Skills: A Primer.* New York: Random, 1989.

Rosenthal, Robert, and Lenore Jacobson. *Pygmalion in the Classroom: Teacher Expectation and Pupils' Intellectual Development.* New York: Holt, 1968.

Rowan, Brian. "Research on Learning and Teaching in K-12 Schools: Implications for the Field of Educational Administration." *Educational Administration Quarterly* 31 (1995): 115-133.

Rowe, Mary Budd. "Wait-Time and Rewards as Instructional Variables, Their Influence on Language, Logic, and Fate Control: Part One – Wait-Time." *Journal of Research in Science Teaching* 11.2 (1974): 81-94.

Wittrock, Merlin C., ed. *Handbook of Research on Teaching.* 3rd ed. New York: Macmillan, 1986.

## Source for Introductory Quote

Rogers, Will. quote. 25 Feb. 2004 <http://www.isl.websearch.com/_1_2NGTUGSOY3KYZ4_websrch.barweb.1/dog/result?otmpl+d>.

# 7

# Effective Testing

The efforts under way in every state to reform education policy and practice through the implementation of higher standards for students and teachers have focused to a large extent on assessment, resulting in a major increase in the amount of testing and in the emphasis placed on its results

*- Education Week, 1999*

It is not surprising many teachers feel inept in designing tests and measuring performance. Education programs have been lax in requiring students to take courses in measurement and assessment. They have also paid little attention to test development in the methods courses taught to pre-service teachers. Many of the state agencies that certify teachers do not even require competency in tests and measurement and as a result, many teachers have limited knowledge about test construction and analysis. Many researchers have documented this training oversight. Jett and Schafer, for example, surveyed Maryland high school teachers and found that twenty percent had no training in classroom assessment, while 40 percent had taken only had one course, part of one course, or an in-service course (71). These findings are consistent with comments made by library media specialists who complain they know little about how to assess students. This chapter presents an overview on the basics of testing to whet the appetite of practitioners who want to know more.

Effective testing involves four stages. The first stage is to write clear objectives for a unit or lesson. A good objective will suggest how it could be tested. Stage two is teaching the lesson in a manner that enables students to learn what will be tested and to suggest to the teacher ways to refine test items. The third stage is administering the test while carefully observing students as they take it, watching for behavior that indicates illness, stress, or distraction. The room where a test is taken should be at a comfortable temperature and have adequate lighting. The fourth and final stage is a careful analysis of each student's performance. Determining how many points each student made may be the initial analysis, but it is less important than determining what each student missed. Determining what students missed is vital to good teaching because it suggests how the lesson needs to be improved and where further instruction is needed.

## Definition of Terms

It is important to understand the language of testing. Although the terms "testing," "evaluation," and "measurement" are used as synonyms, they are different. Robert F. Mager, whose humorous but informative books have taught many people the fundamentals of test construction, defines these three terms in the following manner (8):

- "Measurement is a process of determining the extent of some characteristic associated with an object or person."
- "Evaluation is the act of comparing a measurement with a standard and passing judgment on the comparison."
- "Test is an event during which someone is asked to demonstrate some aspect of his knowledge or skill."

The distinguishing words in these definitions are "process," "act," and "event." Perhaps the following examples will clarify the differences. One measures the size of a room. You test to see if the wall paint is washable. You evaluate whether the room is attractive according to good design principles. From a classroom point of view, you test a student's performance on specific content or skill, the test score is a measure showing how well the student performed on specific criteria, and comparing one student's score against the scores of others is a way to evaluate if the student fits above the norm, or below the norm. To repeat the differences, a test is a one-time event, the outcome of the test is a measurement, and an evaluation compares one performance against other performances or a standard.

## Three Types of Tests

The three types of tests used most often in schools are standardized, summative, and formative. Although newspapers and the public dwell on standardized tests, this type of test was not even used until the mid-19th century. According to *Testing in American Schools*, standardized tests were first administered in Massachusetts as a way to monitor school systems (NRC 25), not students. Today their use in schools to test students is pervasive; some people would say intrusive. Student scores are used to evaluate schools and school systems. These scores have been used as reasons to force change in both organization and curriculum in a school or system. Despite the public's attention to standardized test scores, summative and formative tests contribute more to teaching and learning because they are based on the curriculum taught in a school, the results are available in a timely fashion, and the outcomes help improve future lessons. Aptitude and attitude measures are also used but will not be addressed in this chapter. Table 7.1 gives an overview of the three types of tests, shows the population compared, and states how the results are used. The following sections address each type of test in greater detail.

| Table 7.1 | | | |
|---|---|---|---|
| **Comparison of Three Types of Tests** | | | |
| | **Formative Test** | **Summative Test** | **Standardized Test** |
| *Based Upon* | Specific, limited content | Broader content restricted to an area of study | Broad, general knowledge |
| *Compares* | Classmates | Classes | Population segment, schools |
| *Used to* | Improve learning of content | Pass/fail students | Compare performance Evaluate programs |
| *Results focus on* | Student | Student, Teacher | Student, Teacher, Principal |

## *Standardized Tests*

These tests are called high-stakes because they are used to judge the success or failure of classrooms and schools. This practice is questionable because these tests are based on a broad curriculum instead of what students were actually taught and they are used to measure the performance of a general population. Though it may be useful to compare school performances, standardized tests should be seen for what they are, a broad indicator of how one group is achieving when compared with similar groups, not to evaluate an organization's performance. An official with the National Education Association reminds us, "When tests are punitive, all the attention is focused on the scores. That doesn't help us educate our children" (8). Lipsitz and Mizell criticize standardized tests because they believe scores "may be proxies for student performance, but they reveal little about what students actually know and can do," and this is the real value of a test (533). Recognizing public perception about the importance of these tests, a faculty should examine the objectives on which a standardized test is based to see if those objectives align with the instructional objectives used in the school program.

The format used for most standardized tests is multiple-choice answers. A student's score is usually based on the number of correct choices. Some tests penalize students for guessing by charging the number of wrong answers against the total of right answers so it is important for students to know whether wrong attempts will count against them.

In trying to improve these tests, some vendors have begun to offer a more complex choice of answers. Traditionally, each item had one correct answer and the student selected a letter or number to indicate her choice. Now instead of selecting A, B, C, or D, the choices may be A and C, A and B, or B and C. Test companies now include items that test procedures, not just facts. The following example is a process item.

Choose the correct stage of development for the butterfly.

  a) larva, pupa, egg, butterfly
  b) egg, larva, pupa, butterfly
  c) egg, pupa, larva, butterfly
  d) pupa, egg, larva, butterfly

Some test companies also use negative stems so the students must select the answer that is NOT correct. The negative word in the stem may be highlighted or it may not be. Items with negative stems are scattered among those with positively-stated stems so students must learn to read the items carefully. Today, standardized tests use graphics as test items so students must be able to read and interpret charts and graphs correctly.

There are also standardized writing assessments that are performance-based measures. A common prompt stimulates the students to write and a rubric is used to score each passage. The rubric is used to judge overall development of the passage, organization, support of details, sentence structure, word choice, and mechanics such as spelling and punctuation.

## Summative Tests

These tests are given at the end of instruction; it may be the end of a unit, or a grading period, a semester, or a year. A summative test measures how much a student has learned about a course over a period of time. When the same test is given to several classes, a teacher can compare class performance although care must be taken because class groups are rarely equivalent! Administrators have used summative measures to judge teachers, but this use is unreliable because of differences among class groups. The only way to measure teacher effectiveness is to ensure that student ability in the classes was equivalent. The true worth of a summative test is to determine whether instruction was effective and whether students learned the material deemed most important by an instructor.

## Formative Tests

Formative tests are given as part of instructions. These tests are criterion-referenced, meaning they are based on course objectives the teacher believed a student should have learned from a lesson or lessons. Depending on student performance, a teacher can adjust instruction, repeat portions of the content, or revise techniques and materials. The clearer the objectives, the better the test. The better the test, the more the teacher learns about how well the students understand the lesson. Research has repeatedly shown that using formative tests results to adjust instruction improves student performance if feedback shows each student how to improve (NRC 235). Formative tests allow a teacher to:

• Monitor student progress,
• Catch learning errors, and
• Provide feedback in a timely manner.

Tests results need to be used in at least two ways to take full advantage of the information gained through testing. First, the results determine what content or skills students have or have not learned. Secondly, tests can help teachers understand how students derived the answers they gave and why they made performance errors. Too often the second aspect of testing goes unnoticed. When a teacher reports that 70 percent of his students scored a passing grade, the comment does not provide much insight or analysis. It is important for a teacher to know how each individual performed, reached the answers they gave, and how many of them achieved the course objectives. Analysis should be as routine as scoring a test. One score is just one example of a student's work. Effective assessment is ongoing and should involve numerous samples of a student's knowledge.

# Test Development

Designing a test is complex and difficult because a good test is valid, clearly and correctly stated, and appropriate for the student. A valid test matches the instructional objectives for the lesson or unit. In fact, the teacher should refer to a copy of the test to be certain each lesson covers all pertinent points. Reviewing a test as content covered also provides the instructor with opportunities to spot errors in content or construction. Linn and Gronlund use the fanciful term, WYTIWYG, meaning "what you test is what you get" (98). This device stresses the importance of preparing a valid test, which means the test is consistent with the teaching objectives, and the questions are suited to the maturity level and vocabulary of the students. In other words, a valid test measures what the test developer intended.

Clarity is the second factor important in test development. Errors frequently found in tests, particularly paper and pencil tests, include excessive wordiness, ambiguous stems, items that provide clues to the answer, improper arrangement of items on the test, answers that fall into a pattern, answers that are plausible, and instances of bias. Two flagrant errors that should be avoided at all costs are unclear directions and inadequate time allotment (Linn and Gronlund 100). Writing clear directions is also an important aspect of test development. If an item is constructed in such a manner that a student who really knows the information misses it, the item is not clearly constructed. Likewise, if a student who does not know the information can guess the correct answer because of a construction clue, the item lacks clarity.

Bennion's rules for test construction (42-44) begin with selecting a test format that most readily measures the teaching objectives. Secondly, prepare the test early using no more than three types of items on a test so directions are concise. Prepare a scoring key, a rubric, or an answer sheet when the test is developed instead of just before the test is graded (42-44).

Once a test is constructed, it is reexamined to make certain the directions are clear, language and grammar are correct, items do not signal the answers, and the language is not vague or misleading.

Developing a skill or performance test requires a measure that assesses the learner's performance of the action or procedure at the desired level of proficiency or speed. Or where applicable, producing a product that meets desired standards (Ehrenberg 39). Observation is the most frequently used technique to test a skill, but when a product results from using the skill, it would require measuring the products' worth. For example, a test to determine if a student can locate a library item on a specific topic could be conducted by simple observation. However, a test to determine if a student could plan and execute an Internet search on a specific topic would require two measures, one test would concern search skills and the second would judge the worth of search results.

To develop a performance test requires analyzing the steps used in completing the task to be tested. Next, consider how performance is different when an expert and a novice does it. For example, when an experienced online searcher performs a search she quickly revises it to take advantage of database characteristics or switches databases. Write each step of a process in the correct order to use as a checklist when students demonstrate the skill. A checklist can be upgraded to a rating scale by establishing a continuum for each step of the procedure. Instead of just placing a check to indicate whether or not a student performed a step, the observer would mark whether the performance was a 0 for inadequate, a 5 for proficient, or any number in between. A rating scale can be further developed as a rubric. To transform a rating scale into a rubric requires establishing a standard for exemplary performance for each step of the process. Then adjust the standard so it is less demanding for each descending point on the scale.

It seems especially important for library media specialists to know about checklists, rating scales, and rubrics because they are ways to test many information literacy objectives. Rubistar, a Web site supported by the U.S. Department of Education, assists educators in developing rubrics <http://rubistar.4teachers.org/>. Donham and Stein suggest three considerations when using a rubric. They are to

- Give the rubric to students before they are assessed so they know what is expected.
- Use a rubric repeatedly because this gives students opportunities to improve.
- Use rubrics for complex tasks; a checklist or rating scale is better for simple tasks (216).

Comprehension questions are another useful test format. There are several guidelines to use when writing comprehension questions. The most important consideration is to ask questions in the same order as the information was presented. Ask main idea questions first and then ask for supporting details. Do not ask questions about insignificant points and limit the number of questions asking for specific dates and names, unless those are important points in understanding the topic. When possible, begin a question with a key word that will trigger an answer, such as who, where, how, and why. Reread comprehension questions several times to eliminate vague or confusing language.

There are many types of tests, and just as the preceding paragraphs suggest, each has its own design consideration. Table 7.2 provides an overview of four test categories and lists types of tests within each category. Most of these techniques can be used to assess information literacy objectives, although some are better than others.

| Table 7.2 | |
|---|---|
| **Testing Techniques** | |
| **Paper and Pencil Tests**<br>Multiple Choice<br>Fill-in-the-blank<br>True/False<br>Matching<br>Completion<br>Sentence stems<br>Anecdotal reports<br>Incident reports<br>Pictorial items<br>Arrangement items | **Skill Tests**<br>Demonstration<br>Checklist<br>Rating form<br>Statistics<br>Construction of graphs or models<br>Use of equipment<br>Performance<br>Behavior observation<br>Evaluation form |
| **Essay Questions**<br>Comparison of two things<br>For or against<br>Cause & Effect<br>Explanation<br>Summary<br>Analysis<br>Reorganization of facts<br>Statement of relationship<br>Criticism<br>Discussion<br>Essays with prompt<br>Essays without prompt | **Creative Product Tests**<br>Product evaluation<br>Analogy<br>Portfolio<br>Interview<br>Illustration<br>Oral presentation |

Sources: (Bennion 76-83) (Moore 100-104)

# Testing Is Changing

More attention is being given to testing as more has been learned about human cognition. Tests are improving because they are now student-centered instead of teacher-centered, they test process as well as product, they vary in testing mode, and they allow more than one correct answer.

Today the emphasis has shifted "from an accumulation of isolated facts and skills to an emphasis on the application and use of knowledge" (Herman, Aschbacher, and Winters 13). Consider the wonderful example found on page 28 in *Knowing What Students Know*. Two students are asked, "What was the date of the battle of the Spanish Armada?" The first student responds, "1588," a correct answer. The second student fits the event into context, saying

> "It must have been around 1590. I know the English began to settle in Virginia just after 1600, not sure of the exact date. They wouldn't have dared start overseas exploration if Spain still had control of the seas. It would take a little while to get expeditions organized, so England must have gained naval supremacy somewhere in the late 1500s."

Although the first student might get a better grade, there seems little doubt the second student has a better understanding of the historical period. As educators, our task is to be able to formulate questions and assessment tasks that call forth reasoned instead of rote responses.

Educators know tests need to do more than just determine whether students can recognize or recall basic facts. They know tests must call for higher order thinking. Paula Cannon, Math Specialist at the Alabama Department of Education, illustrated how a basic skill item could be adjusted to measure higher order thinking. The basic skill item uses a pie chart showing distribution of Jane's weekly income. Various sized pieces of the pie show the percentage spent on groceries, rent, etc. However, the piece labeled "savings" shows no percentage. The student is asked to determine what percentage of Jane's income is savings. A higher-order-thinking item could use the same pie chart but students would be asked to determine how much Jane saves each week if her weekly income is $432. Whether on written exams or in oral responses, teachers are learning how to cause students to think. Black and Wiliam report observing a teacher who reversed the age-old pattern of asking a question, student responding, ask a second question, student responding. Instead, this teacher asks a question and calls on a student but directs the student to discuss his answer with a fellow student before responding. The teacher did not reply whether the answer was right or wrong, but instead asked the student to explain how he and his classmate reached their answer. After their explanation, other students were asked if they agreed or disagreed and why (qtd in NRC 226-227).

A report from California explains how scenarios were used as a device to assess information skills in competence. The scenarios were real-life situations to make them more authentic tests and to underscore the relationship between skills learned in school and real-life experiences. An example of a scenario was as an individual "… working in a group to study the homeless in your community. Your task is to inform the City Council on the current state of homelessness." Two associated questions were: "What type of information do you need to know?" and "How would you use this information to help describe the state of the homeless?" (Dunn 26-36). Although educators are paying more attention to test development and they are improving, developing a test remains a complex and demanding task.

## Information Literacy Tests

As with any test, an information literacy test must be based on instructional objectives. The language of an objective sets parameters for the test item. The first step in writing a test item is to examine the verb used in the objective because it usually states the behavior expected of the learner. Verbs frequently found in information skill objectives are "use," "identify," "compare," and "recognize." Each verb suggests considerations for item construction. For example, use suggests a performance test such as using encyclopedias, almanacs, or online databases. Identify requires a student to define and describe the pertinent characteristics and to be able to distinguish an example from non-examples. A student could select a description, recall the description, write a definition, or identify the correct item among several shown. Compare requires two or more examples in order to show likeness and differences. Recognize is a low-level measure because it is easier to recognize a correct answer than it is to recall it. However, if a student is asked to recognize bias or a flawed argument, the task is really evaluation, which is a high-level task.

The following examples illustrate how a test item is tied to an instructional objective. Read the objective, focus on the active verb in the objective, and then see if the test item would cause a student to do what the objective states.

### Kindergarten

*Instructional Objective:* Describe characters in a story.

Test Items:    Show a picture of a book character for children to describe.
Say an adjective and ask the children to relate it to a character in the book.
Place pictures of book characters on a table and ask students to identify those who are the most alike, e.g. solve a problem, help others, etc.

### Grade 2

*Instructional Objective:* Use an encyclopedia to locate facts about people, places and things.

Test Item:    Write the name of a place, person, or thing on each note card. Ask students to write the letter where information about the item could be found in a printed encyclopedia. Distribute 10 cards to each student.

### Grade 4

*Instructional Objective:* Summarize information from written passages.

Test Item:    Give the same passage to every student. Ask the student to highlight the most important points and then to restate those points in a paragraph.

### Grade 6

*Instructional Objective:* Retrieve information from grids, schedules, and tables.

Test Item:    Give each student a bus schedule and have them plan transportation to school from point A to point B (using local destinations).

### Grade 9

*Instructional Objective:* Evaluate the use of slang, dialect, imagery, and dialogue in a novel.

Test Item:     Give each student the same narrative passage to analyze and evaluate. Have them label instances of these literary elements.

### Grade 12

*Instructional Objective:* Locate financial and business information collected by the federal government.

Test Item:     Give each student a different problem statement concerning information that might be needed by a family or individual. Without suggesting appropriate sites, ask the students to locate online information from a government-sponsored source, to cite the source, and state the information in a form that would be useable by the average citizen.

# Checklist for Effective Testing

- The assessment clearly reflects lesson/unit objectives.
- Students understand what will be tested.
- The test is appropriate to the type and scope of the instruction.
- The test is appropriate to the age of the students.
- The length of the test suits the testing period and age of the student.
- Each point is assessed more than once to be certain a correct answer is not obtained by chance.
- Over time, a variety of test formats are used.
- Test results are considered as only one example of what the student knows or can do.
- Test results will be analyzed to determine changes needed in the instructional plan.
- Follow-up questions determine if test items were misinterpreted or not understood.

# Sources Cited

Bennion, Donald H. *Assessing Student Learning: Behavioral Objectives and Evaluation Procedures for the Affective, Cognitive and Psychomotor Domains.* Dubuque, IA: Kendall/Hunt, 1977.

Donham, Jean, and Barbara Barnard Stein. "Assessment: A Tool for Developing Lifelong Learners." Barbara K. Stripling, Ed. *Learning and Libraries in an Information Age: Principles and Practice.* Englewood, CO: Libraries Unlimited, 1999. 206-228.

Dunn, Kathleen. "Assessing Information Literacy Skills in the California State University: A Progress Report." *Journal of Academic Librarianship* 28.1/2 (2002): 26-36.

Ehrenberg, Sydelle D. "Concept Learning: How to Make It Happen in the Classroom." *Educational Leadership* 39.1 (1981): 36-43.

Herman, Joan L., Pamela R. Aschbacher, and Lynn Winters. *A Practical Guide to Alternative Assessment.* Alexandria, VA: ASCD, 1992.

Jett, Daniel L., and William D. Schafer. "Ready or Not, Teachers K-12 Move to Center Stage in the Assessment Arena: Implications for State Education Policymakers." *Measurement & Evaluation in Counseling & Development* 26.1 (1993): 69-81.

Linn, Robert L., and Norman E. Gronlund. *Measurement and Assessment in Teaching.* 8th ed. Upper Saddle River, NJ: Prentice-Hall, 1999.

Lipsitz, Joan, and M. Hayes Mizell. "Speaking with One Voice: A Manifesto for Middle-Grades Reform." *Phi Delta Kappan* 78.7 (1997): 533-540.

Mager, Robert F. *Measuring Instructional Intent or Got a Match?* Belmont, CA: Fearon, 1973.

Moore, Kenneth D. *Classroom Teaching Skills: A Primer.* New York: Random, 1989.

National Education Association. "High-Stakes Questions." Cover Story. *NEA Today* Mar. (2003): 8-11.

National Research Council. Committee on the Foundations of Assessment. James W. Pelligrino, Naomi Chudowsky, and Robert Glaser. Eds. *Knowing What Students Know: The Science of Design of Educational Assessment.* Washington, DC: Natl. Acad., 2001.

# 8
# Teaching and Testing Information Literacy

> If you don't have a strategy, you will be permanently reactive and part of somebody else's strategy.
>
> *- Alvin Toffler*

One reason a library media specialist is interrupted several times a day could be that teachers and principals do not understand the benefits of the media program. They may think a media specialist is just sitting and waiting to be asked to do something constructive, particularly when they walk by the media center and on the surface nothing appears to be happening. Toffler's quote sends an important message: have a strategy and broadcast how it benefits the school!

Teaching is certainly an important part of a media specialist's job—perhaps the most engaging part—but it is not the only job that must be done. Time must also be allocated for management and collection responsibilities. Teachers and many administrators do not understand these responsibilities. With a positive attitude, find a way to show them the tasks that must be accomplished and help them understand the approximate time each task requires. Make your case, but make it brief and to the point.

Effective time management contributes to overall media center operation. It is also important in planning and delivering instruction. This chapter presents the eight steps used in planning a lesson effectively and efficiently. These steps are relevant whether planning is done collaboratively or by yourself in the media center.

# Getting Ready to Teach and Test

Four things need to be in place before a media specialist is ready to plan, teach, and test. Those things are to:

- Have a structured information literacy curriculum,
- Know the school's curriculum,
- Identify ways to integrate information skills into the teaching program, and
- Elicit support from the administration and teachers (at least a few).

With this foundation, library media specialists can engage in planning instruction with classroom teachers or teaching teams. The outcome of this effort must be clearly communicated to the administration, faculty, and parents. When their students learn to use information, it will improve their classroom and test performance. To make that promise come true, there must be a plan with structured lessons. Each lesson is developed by:

- Identifying objectives,
- Specifying prerequisites,
- Generating learning activities,
- Meeting individual needs,
- Selecting resources,
- Providing practice opportunities,
- Choosing an assessment method, and
- Scheduling space, time, and personnel.

Each step is briefly covered in the following sections. The chapter ends with a planning form and five sample lessons.

## Identifying Objectives

Objectives show the purpose for instruction. They specify the content, skill, or attitude the student must acquire. Sometimes an objective statement will also specify the expected level of performance and/or resources to be used. Compare the following examples:

- The student will be able to identify the capitals of the 50 U.S. states.
- The student will be able to use an atlas in identifying the capitals of the 50 U.S. states.
- The student will be able to identify the capitals of at least 30 of the 50 U.S. states.

Care must be taken by a lesson planner to be certain all objectives do not just target acquisition of basic facts. Students should be challenged by moving them from learning to recall facts to function at a more sophisticated stage of thinking. Benjamin Bloom's taxonomy helps guide teachers in planning instruction over time so students move from simple to more complex learning, such as interpretation, application, and synthesis. Media specialists who want to know more about Bloom's work will be interested in two books. In *InfoQuest: A New*

*Twist on Information Literacy*, Peggy Milam provides examples of student behavior for each of Bloom's six stages of learning, and suggests stems for generating activities (54-55). An example in her book explains how a student conducting an analysis might need to compare, contrast, examine, investigate, separate, or categorize. A book that is particularly useful for media specialists who seek help in translating objectives into learning activities is Eisenberg and Berkowitz's *Curriculum Initiative: An Agenda and Strategy for Library Media Programs* (103). This book provides a list of questions linked to each of Bloom's cognitive levels. For example, questions related to analysis include

- "What is the main idea …?"
- "What word appropriately describes …?"
- "Find evidence that indicates …"

Objective statements should be specific because broad objectives result in a muddled instructional plan. "The student will be able to write a good paragraph" is less specific than "the student will be able to write a paragraph that supports the topic sentence."

Certain objectives are more important or essential than others because these are objectives everyone must achieve. The teacher needs to highlight these essential objectives for the class. Learning activities must be planned to teach, test, and re-teach essential objectives until all students have grasped them. Which of the four objectives that follow would be essential in a lesson on national parks?

- Identify and locate five national parks or monuments.
- Explain how national parks and monuments are designated.
- Identify the first U.S. national park and the year it was designated.
- Identify and locate national parks and monuments in our state.

If the focus of instruction is government, the second objective could be judged essential, but if the lesson were part of a unit on the state, the fourth objective would be the most important. There are no hard and fast rules that dictate which objectives are essential, but a teacher knows the objectives that form a basis for future study and those objectives that will be tested.

### Specifying Prerequisites

Many objectives require preliminary skill or knowledge. For example, a student must know what a topic sentence is before being able to write supporting sentences. A teacher must ensure each student has prerequisite knowledge before initiating more advanced study. Usually one or two students in a class will lack the needed prerequisite knowledge or skill. This situation presents an instructional problem because a teacher finds it hard to justify teaching two students while others wait. If the teacher elects to move on, often the two students will fall further behind. Media specialists can help alleviate these situations by providing space and supervision for the two students to get remediation in the media center with instruction provided by peers or computers.

## Generating Learning Activities

This phase of lesson planning requires thinking outside the box so the same activities are not repeated lesson after lesson. Too much instruction consists of lecture and answering questions. While didactic instruction has its place, there is too much telling and "seat work" in today's classroom. Remember the quote by Will Rogers at the beginning of chapter six that stressed the importance of engaging eyes as well as ears when teaching—the same could be said about engaging hands.

A media specialist, particularly one with little teaching experience or training, may find it useful to have on hand a list of verbs to help generate activities related to an objective. For example, an objective that calls for students to discriminate between two or more items might be reached through activities that involve choosing, comparing, contrasting, deciding, detecting, differentiating, judging, or pairing. An objective where students must apply a rule could involve calculating, concluding, constructing, designing, estimating, extrapolating, illustrating, or interpreting. Some media specialists, particularly those new at planning instruction may turn to published sources for ideas. There are many books currently available that involve a range of subject areas. Books such as:

- *Flip It* by Alice Yucht
- *InfoQuest* by Peggy Milam
- *Social Studies Discoveries on the Net* by Anthony Fredericks
- *Soaring Through the Universe: Astronomy through Children's Literature* by Joanne Letwinch
- *Teacher's Weather Sourcebook: Information, Ideas, and Activities* by Tom Konvicka
- *Exploring Science in the Library: Resources and Activities for Young People* edited by Tracy Gath and Maria Sosa
- *Information Skills Toolkit: Collaborative Integrated Instruction for the Middle Grades* by Debra Kay Logan.

Whether you consult idea books or a list of verbs, the more you generate activities, the easier it becomes. Activities planned for a lesson one year become the basis for planning the following year, although the same activities should not be used year after year.

## Meeting Individual Needs

Lessons will be more successful when the instructor accommodates the learning needs of students. Rita and Kenneth Dunn studied innate learning preferences of individuals and found there are 23 elements that affect a person's ability to absorb, process, and retain information. They grouped these elements into five categories

- Environmental,
- Emotional,
- Sociological,
- Physical, and
- Psychology.

In class, these differences are evident in student behavior. Some students can sit still for a long time while others cannot concentrate unless they can move about. Some students learn best when the light is bright while others are distracted by abundant light. Some students learn best by hearing information, while many learn best by seeing it, and some learn best by manipulating it. The Center for the Study of Learning and Teaching Styles has developed five measures to help teachers determine student learning preferences. Teachers who have used these measures and then accommodated the learning styles of their students have been rewarded with improved student performance (qtd. in Dunn and Smith).

Suppose an essential objective was for every student to be able to label all 50 states with the appropriate two-letter abbreviation. A range of learning activities would accommodate various preferences. Consider the following list of activities to accommodate various learning styles:

- Write the correct abbreviation for each state on the worksheet map of the U.S.
- Match cards with the state name, shape, and abbreviation.
- Complete a puzzle of the U.S. where each piece shows the abbreviation.
- Fill-in an outline map posted on the wall using the correct abbreviation.
- Name the state as the corresponding abbreviation is shown.
- Cut out a pattern for every state and label it with the appropriate abbreviation.
- Alphabetize 50 cards with abbreviations representing each state.

Some activities require students to remain seated while one requires moving about. Some activities require students to manipulate puzzle pieces or scissors, but all engage students in active learning. Except for the writing activity, students are not just sitting and soaking up information. This example shows how students can work in different ways toward the same objective.

## Selecting Resources

In some instances an objective specifies the type of resource needed, but in other instances a variety of resources may be appropriate. When planning lessons, teachers are often willing for the library media specialist to take the lead in this task. When this happens, it is a golden opportunity to inform teachers about relevant resources that have not been used or to inform them about pertinent new resources. This planning stage provides opportunities to underscore the advantage of using various resources in more than one mode. Always review resources before using them in a classroom situation to be certain they are error-free, unbiased, clear, creditable, and well-paced.

When using media in a lesson, consider the impact that rate of presentation can have. Presentation rate involves both the speed of words spoken or scrolled on screen and the speed of ideas presented. Both factors affect the amount of information a student receives. Materials packed with information need to be accompanied by some type of graphic organizer to help students follow along.

## Planning Practice Opportunities

Practice provides students with opportunities to perfect a skill, to retain knowledge, and to build competence. It also provides instructors with an opportunity to determine if a student can perform or has learned correctly. Practice opportunities should be monitored carefully at first so the instructor can correct any mistakes. As the student gains competence, practice becomes more independent. Eventually, the conditions surrounding practice can be altered or varied because students will be skilled or knowledgeable enough to adjust to the new situation.

### Choosing a Test

Classroom assessments let an instructor know which students have learned the specified objectives, although the teacher is also tested in a classroom assessment. When a teacher sees poor results as simply an indictment of the students, he misses the point. A well-constructed test reveals not only what students have failed to learn, but it also shows where teaching failed and why students made errors.

An appropriate test measures the skill or knowledge specified in the instructional objective. An appropriate test for shooting a basketball or making a cake is not writing descriptions of these procedures, but demonstrating them. When students have studied the Great Depression, it is not appropriate to give them a test on stock market fundamentals.

### Scheduling Space, Time, and Personnel

These housekeeping details do not take much planning time, but it is important to the flow of instruction for them to be clearly designated. Nothing is more frustrating than having a group of students come to the media center expecting a lesson only to find it is the wrong day, or for the media specialist to prepare materials for 10 students instead of 12.

Check to make certain that space, time, and responsibilities are clearly communicated. Make notes about space, time, and personnel on the planning sheet. While format and neatness are not essential, a clear understanding of who is doing what is. Complete plans result in good lessons.

# Keeping Records

Good records are valuable accountability measures and reminders of what has been done. It is important to keep a record or calendar showing when teachers were contacted and when planning was completed. It is easy for two or three teachers to slip through the net, and before you know it, much of the school year is gone and the students in those classes have not been instructed in information literacy skills. Two ways to keep these records is to use a wall chart in the media office or on the computer. At the end of each unit or semester or school year, ask teachers to complete a quick and easy evaluation form about the planning activity to determine problems or to solicit suggestions for improvement. Selected portions of this data can also be used in the media center's annual report.

It is too cumbersome for a media specialist to keep a record for each student but there should be a record of the objectives taught to each class throughout the year. A second important record to maintain is a file with copies of the plans made with every teacher or lessons taught to each class. Eisenberg and Berkowitz suggest several record keeping options in *Curriculum Initiative: An*

*Agenda and Strategy for Library Media Programs* (Ch. 8 and 11), and Smith provides record keeping forms in Appendix C in *Achieving a Curriculum-Based Library Media Center Program: The Middle School Model for Change.* Milam's book, in chapter 16 on program assessment, offers a variety of forms that can be adapted for record-keeping purposes.

# Finding Time for Planning

Most schools have workdays before the school year begins and occurring regularly throughout the school year, days when students do not attend. These days are opportunities to meet with teachers or teaching teams to set a schedule for information literacy activities. In an ideal situation, a planning schedule would be routine because collaborative planning would occur at regular intervals. However, even lacking that level of implementation, it is possible to schedule information literacy planning and instruction. To take advantage of planning opportunities requires the media specialist to know what teachers will teach in the coming months and being ready to tie information literacy skills to those topics. This point has been made several times in this book but it is worth repeating.

Again, in the best of worlds, a media specialist would plan collaboratively with every teacher. In the real world, the media specialist will plan with teachers who are willing. Regardless, library media specialists must move ahead in teaching all students because our challenge is to reach all students. At a minimum, the media specialist's goal is to teach the information literacy objectives listed in the curriculum for each grade and to show students how to use those skills in their coursework.

Library media specialists are urged to take the lead in implementing an information literacy curriculum. It is a demanding task considering all the other responsibilities expected, but media specialists are in the best position to do it due to their background information and training. Often teachers and administrators are uncertain about the media specialist's role and some educators are even unsure of what name to use when referring to the position. A media specialist must work for successful implementation because professional standards expect students and staff to acquire skill in accessing, evaluating, and using information and reaching this goal requires interaction with students and teachers. Professional expectations challenge each library media specialist to communicate effectively, to understand the school's instructional program, and to sell the faculty on the benefits of collaborative planning and integrating information skill development into coursework.

The checklist that follows is adapted from one that Dr. Kent Gustafson, a noted instructional design authority, included in an article written for the 1990 *School Library Media Annual.* It is a useful tool for checking instructional plans to make certain they cover essential elements. This chapter ends by presenting samples of completed planning forms and lesson plans. The last chapter reveals the experiences of two middle school media specialists who practice what this book preaches. They plan collaboratively with teachers so students learn information skills as they learn course content. As you might expect, not everything goes smoothly!

# Checklist for Instructional Planning

*Kent L. Gustafson*

| Events | Suggested Questions |
|---|---|
| **Check Readiness** | Does the learner have the needed skills/knowledge?<br>How will readiness be checked?<br>How will the learner be told the purpose of the lesson? |
| **Present Instruction** | What is the appropriate physical rate of presentation?<br>What is the appropriate substantive rate of presentation?<br>How can content be organized to facilitate retention?<br>What materials will be used to supplement the textbook?<br>What will be done to engage the learners? |
| **Guide Learning** | What accommodations are made for diverse learners?<br>What structure is provided to help students learn?<br>Have distracting and unnecessary stimuli been eliminated? |
| **Elicit Performance** | Is practice consistent with the objective?<br>Is practice required to gain proficiency or to promote recall?<br>Is the form of practice varied to prevent boredom? |
| **Provide Feedback** | Is feedback provided in a timely manner?<br>Is the feedback clear?<br>If needed, is additional instruction available? |
| **Assess Performance** | What is the appropriate form of assessment?<br>Is the assessment consistent with the objective?<br>Is the assessment consistent with instruction?<br>Is the assessment valid and reliable? |
| **Enhance Transfer** | Has transfer been modeled for students?<br>What activities promote transfer and generalization? |

Adapted with permission from Dr. Gustafson

# Sample Unit Plan

**Subject Area**  Social Studies, Era of Global War, 1914 to 1945
**Planning Date**  October 7, 2004

**Classroom Teacher**  J. Cooper, Room 15

**Time Period of the Unit**  Nov. 3–Dec. 15

## Unit Goal(s)
- To think critically about the forces that combine to shape the world.
- To compare and contrast conditions and outcomes.

## Instructional Objectives
- Analyze the causes, course, and consequences of WW I.
- Explain the rise of communism in Russia.
- Assess the challenges of the post WW I period.
- Evaluate the causes and global impact of the Great Depression.
- Analyze causes, course, and consequences of WW II.

## Information Objectives
- Research events occurring in a specific time period.
- Compare and contrast information found in two or more sources.
- Distinguish fact from opinion.
- Use historical maps to locate information.

## Proposed Strategies
- Teams
- View movies to gain information and develop rapport.
- Timeline development.
- Letter writing or newspaper of the time

## Proposed Activities
- Interview people who lived through the Depression.
- Team for WW I and WW II to research and report.
- Compare causes of WW I and WW II.
- Read books set in one of the war periods.
- Research the lives of leaders during the period.
- Classify common experiences of leaders.

## Proposed Evaluation
- Theme describing life during WW I, WW II, or the Great Depression.
- Rubric used for self-evaluation, peer evaluation, and teacher evaluation.

# Sample Lesson Plan

**Classroom Teacher**  J. Cooper          **Date of Activity**  Thursday, Nov. 20

**Unit**   Era of Global War, 1914 to 1945

**Strategy**  Team research

**Activity**  Consequence of WW I and WW II
(Specify action and person responsible for each section)

**Introduction**  Teacher responsible
  • Explain activity's purpose, expected outcome, and evaluative measure

**Determine Past Knowledge** Media Specialist responsible
  • Questionnaire to determine student knowledge about identifying search terms, writing search statement, and using positional and logical operators.
  (After-school training offered to interested students needing remediation.)

**Resources**
  • Internet
  • Digitized databases
  • Print and media

**Teach (demonstrate, explain)**  Media Specialist
  • Present slide presentation on developing a search strategy.
  • Use video projector to demonstrate a search.

**Practice**  Teacher and Media Specialist
  • Pairs of students are scheduled to use computers in the classroom and in the library.
  • Scheduled team discussion of search results.

**Review**  Student Teams

**Evaluate**  Written exam; Newspaper article written in the time and location assigned, graded with rubric

# Primary Lesson Plan *2nd Grade Physical Education*

**Classroom Teacher** Richardson          **Date of Activity** May 8-13

**Unit** Folk dances

## Strategy
- Learn dances; relate each dance to country, customs, native costumes

## Activity
- Listen to stories and read books set in specific country.
- Draw pictures showing landscape and native dress.

## Introduction
- Teacher will demonstrate dance native to U.S. (western two-step).
- Media specialist shows how western life and dress can be found in books, etc.

## Determine Past Knowledge
- The names of each dance to be learned are written on the white board. Students volunteer what they know about each one, and their comments are written under the appropriate name.

## Resources
- Music
- Books, picture sets, slides

## Teach
- Teacher teaches one dance each day.
- Media specialist features each country in a display surrounded by related resources, reads a story set in each country, and talks about related books students might read.

## Practice
- Students perform each dance and talk about what they have learned about the people and country from media center resources.

## Review
- Questionnaire asks students to match country, dance, and costume.

## Evaluate
- Teacher judges ability of student to do each dance as the class performs.
- Media specialist asks questions about stories read and lists books read by each student.

# Intermediate Lesson Plan *4th Grade Science*

**Classroom Teacher**  Wrobel                **Date of Activity**  Feb. 2-5

**Unit**    Space Study: Planets

**Strategy**
- Use models to show relative size and distance.

**Activity**
- Making models, video, almanac use

**Introduction**
- The class will watch "The Sun: Earth's Star," a video produced by the National Geographic Society. Each student will originate two questions about the video's content.
- Media specialist will review organization of almanac.

**Determine Past Knowledge**
- Student teams will participate in a game show format to answer the student-generated questions.

**Resources**
- Textbook, Video, Art supplies, Web sites

**Teach**
- One group of students will stand on the playground according to the distance of the planets from the sun, holding a poster board model representing the appropriate size of each planet. Distance and size will be accurately scaled using information from the almanac.
- One group of students will make a solar system in the hall by hanging styrofoam balls from the ceiling. Distance and size will be scaled.
- Pairs of students will explore each of the four assigned websites: Space Science, The Nine Planets Tour, Hurricane Storm Science and SpaceLink. Each pair will develop materials that explain what type of information is available and search techniques.

**Practice and Review**
- Students complete and report on projects, working in both the classroom and the media center.

**Evaluation**
- Each student will place planet cutouts in correct order by size and distance from the sun.

# Middle School Lesson Plan *7th Grade English*

**Classroom Teacher**  Holland          **Date of Activity**  Oct. 21-25

**Unit**  Study Skills

## Strategy
- Modeling, transparencies, exercises, PowerPoint illustration

## Introduction
- The media specialist shows a PowerPoint presentation on study skills (note-taking, using location aids, skimming and scanning, outlining, paraphrasing, and summarizing).

## Determine Past Knowledge
- Each student is given the same written passage to read, outline, and summarize within fifteen minutes.

## Resources
- Copies, transparencies, books

## Teach
- The teacher projects a written passage on the screen and models how it could be outlined, paraphrased, and summarized. Students repeat the process with passages on duplicated sheets.
- The media specialist distributes copies of a table of contents and an index to use in quizzing students about page numbers, subheadings, and cross-references.

## Practice
- Students outline, paraphrase, and summarize passages. Their work, without identifying names, is placed on transparencies and shown for class discussion and comparison. Students are each assigned a topic and given 15 minutes to locate three facts in books.

## Review
- A worksheet with two examples of outlines, paraphrases, and summaries to critique.

## Evaluate
- Each student is assigned a topic to research, organize, and write a one-page paper.

# Secondary Lesson Plan  *12th Grade Economics*

**Classroom Teacher**  Valentino                    **Date of Activity**  May 17-19

**Unit**  Macroeconomics

**Strategy**
- Online searching for current government-gathered information

**Activity**
- Demonstration, online searching, computer projection, teams

**Introduction**
- Using computer projection, the media specialist demonstrates points used in evaluating a Web site (authority, scope, content, structure, and search features).

**Determine Past Knowledge**
- Each student is given a paper/pencil test on the content of selected databases.

**Resources**
- Computers, databases, printouts, selected database examples

**Teach**
- Three-member teams develop and present a PowerPoint product to teach other class members about an assigned online database that contains economic information. The media specialist models how to cite an online source.

**Practice**
- Each student is given the task of locating five items of specific data and citing the sources.

**Review**
- A worksheet identifies 10 items of economic information and asks students to select the best online source from several options.

**Evaluate**
- Students must identify the first source they would use to locate specific economic information.

# Sources Cited

American Association of School Librarians, and Association for Educational Communications and Technology. *Information Power: Building Partnerships for Learning*. Chicago: American Library Association, 1998.

Dunn, Rita, and Jane Bandy Smith. "Learning Styles and Library Media Programs." *School Library Media Annual* (8). Ed. Jane Bandy Smith. Englewood, CO: Libraries Unlimited, 1990. 32-49.

Eisenberg, Michael B., and Robert E. Berkowitz. *Curriculum Initiative: An Agenda and Strategy for Library Media Programs*. Norwood, NJ: Ablex, 1990.

---. *Resource Companion to Curriculum Initiative: An Agenda and Strategy for Library Media Programs*. Norwood, NJ: Ablex, 1988.

Gustafson, Kent L. "Designing Effective Instruction: The Events of Instruction." *School Library Media Annual* (8). Ed. Jane Bandy Smith. Englewood, CO: Libraries Unlimited, 1990. 50-58.

Milam, Peggy. *InfoQuest: A New Twist on Information Literacy*. Worthington, OH: Linworth, 2001.

Smith, Jane Bandy. *Achieving a Curriculum-Based Library Media Center Program: The Middle School Model for Change*. Chicago: ALA, 1995: 56.

# Source for Introductory Quote

Toffler, Alvin. *Fortune*. Nov. 22 (1999): 170.

# 9

# Two Middle School Experiences

> By building partnerships with teachers, I find I can better teach skill lessons in a meaningful context, provide greater access to resources, and foster situations that more effectively help students develop the skills they need.
>
> *- Debra Kay Logan*

Earlier chapters show how traditional library skills have broadened to encompass study and thinking skills. The transition to information literacy shifts the emphasis from students being able to access resources to being able to derive meaning from the information they find and to use it in an appropriate manner. This means a student must not only have location skills but must also be able to analyze, evaluate, and organize the information that is found. Students with these skills will be able to remember more and will use information more effectively and efficiently. Having these capabilities is the reason why information literacy can improve student performance in coursework and on tests.

Once a media specialist grasps the information skills that students need to learn and believes those skills will strengthen overall student performance, the most difficult part of the job still lies ahead. Despite the fact that collaboration is mutually beneficial, it is the media specialist who must convince teachers to collaborate so these skills are used routinely as a means of completing class activities. It does not matter where skill instruction occurs. It can take place in the media center, or in the classroom, or in each place at different times. What matters is that students acquire these skills. For this to happen in a proficient manner, skill instruction must be linked with classroom content so students practice information skills while learning course content. This is an essential approach because it makes skill instruction relevant to a student's real world. Earlier chapters have suggested how to encourage teachers to collaborate and have illustrated a process to use in integrating information skills with course content. Armed with this information, it will be helpful to hear from two media specialists who actually used the process in their middle schools. Because a middle school is truly in-between elementary and secondary schools, media specialists at all school levels should be able to relate to their experiences.

Lisa Churchill and Lucy Mason have years of experience in directing middle school media centers. Both are recognized as providing student-centered programs and working collaboratively with classroom teachers. Although they have been in classrooms and media centers in other states and cities, they currently work in schools located south of Birmingham, Alabama. Lisa is employed by the Jefferson County school system, a large system by Alabama standards, it has 65 schools. Lucy works for the Hoover City school system. Hoover is one of the fastest growing communities in Alabama. One indication of the rapid population growth is the number of new schools in the system; four new schools have opened within three years. Located several miles apart, the two middle schools are similar in some ways, and yet as all schools are, different in others.

The same format is used for both reports to enable readers to easily see the commonalities and differences between the two experiences. Readers should remember these reports were written "on the run." Each account begins by describing the school plant, the student body, the cooperating teacher, and the media program. Perhaps the most interesting and illuminating section is the diary each media specialist kept as a record of events that occurred during the collaborative project. These experiences are not presented as exemplary models, if indeed any such collaborative examples exist. Instead, they provide readers with an opportunity to get inside an experienced practitioner's head to understand the uncertainties, frustrations, satisfactions, and yearnings that anyone who tries to implement integrated skill instruction will feel. Lisa and Lucy have been kind enough and open enough to share with the rest of us. For that, we owe them our gratitude.

## Source for Introductory Quote

Logan, Debra Kay. *Information Skills Toolkit: Collaborative Integrated Instruction for the Middle Grades*. Worthington, OH: Linworth, 2000.

# Experience #1

## Gresham Middle School, Jefferson County Schools, Alabama

### Description of School and Students

Every good school has a goal or mission statement and the Gresham Middle School is no exception. Its mission is to teach academics with an emphasis on students becoming independent and responsible citizens. The school community believes this mission can only be achieved in a safe and physically comfortable environment with learning the chief priority. The faculty is committed to seeing that every student becomes confident, self-directed, and prepared to be lifelong learners. They provide the tools students will need to achieve these goals.

Located in a suburb south of Birmingham, the school was built in the 1960s when an open building concept was in vogue. The concept did not prove popular with most teachers, who almost immediately began constructing walls out of bookshelves and bulletin boards. Instead of being a single school building, Gresham has four octagonal buildings clustered together, three of them connected by covered walkways. Despite some drawbacks, the facility offers adequate space for academics, athletics, and fine arts for the 530 students who attend. Although the school has been remodeled to eliminate many of the open building features, the media center remains open. There are no doors for the media center, which creates somewhat of a security problem regarding the collection.

Even though the school is set in an upper income housing area, middle and lower income students are bused in due to school zoning. In recent years, there has been an influx of foreign-born students, mostly from Mexico, South America, and the Far East.

### Description of Cooperating Teacher

Mr. Keith Berry, a science teacher at Gresham Middle School, teaches topics that include astronomy, human body systems, heredity, resources, weather and climate, forces and motion, and chemistry. The last topic was the focus for our collaborative project. Mr. Berry often uses the Socratic method in his classroom. He asks leading questions to which his students must respond using analysis, reasoning, and logic. This approach is challenging but appears to result in more confident students. He requires various academic activities that include individual projects, class projects, hands-on experiences, and Internet research. In the final analysis, his goal is to encourage students to think.

Although new to education, he brings a wealth of information to the classroom because previously he was a scientific researcher at the University of Alabama in Birmingham (UAB). This institution includes a recognized medical center engaged in breakthrough research. Mr. Berry's former job does not go unnoticed by his students who perceive his brilliance and hang on every word. When lecturing, he illustrates points on the blackboard. Mr. Berry's classes are held in a structured learning environment. At one time his classroom was a lab, but now the lab tables and chairs have been replaced by desks placed in rows.

## Library Media Services

The library/media center serves as a major support element for the teaching and learning processes in the school. Each year, the media specialist obtains funds by writing grants and seeking donations to pay for an author's visit to the school. The program is called "Readers Meet Writers in the Middle," which is more than just inviting an author to visit with students at the school. The visit begins with a dinner honoring the author where library media specialists from Birmingham schools are invited to get to know the author. Naturally, the authors selected are those who write books enjoyed by middle school students.

Channel One is another service provided by the media center, and is available in every classroom. Each year the media center sponsors a book fair and an associated program called "Reading Is a Family Affair." Other school programs sponsored by the media center include the spelling bee, poetry festival, cultural awareness program, and a handwriting contest. "Out with the Old and In with the New" is an annual event held at the beginning of each calendar year. This event is an opportunity for the faculty to browse new additions to the collection and to suggest items that should be withdrawn.

## Project Diary

**March 5**  *I invited Mr. Berry to participate in a combined chemistry and information skills unit that would improve his eighth graders' critical thinking skills. After talking with him about information skills for about 10 minutes, I asked to see a copy of the teacher's edition for his class textbook and questioned him about the upcoming chemistry unit. I urged him to consider working with me on the endeavor because the information skills would enable his students to gain more from his lectures on chemistry. I thought my approach was subtle, inviting, and certain to receive an immediate, "yes." Instead he said, "I'll think about it."*

**March 6**  *I dropped by Mr. Berry's room to ask if he had considered our joint venture. He said he was still considering it but asked about the length of the endeavor. I assured him that it would only take a little extra time for a pretest, visits to the media center, and a posttest to see if the literacy skills were learned. I could tell he was busy and so I only took about three minutes to explain my proposition. I said if he would loan me a copy of the student text that I would identify related information skills, prepare a pretest, learning activities, and a posttest. I hoped for a positive response ... he simply stated that he would think about it.*

**March 7**  *After two more days of coaxing, Mr. Berry delivered a copy of the eighth grade science textbook, four pages of information from the Internet on critical thinking skills, and said he was willing and ready to give my proposal a try. He would work with me in both class sections, the 7th period class and the 8th period class. Hurray!*

**March 12**  *Mr. Berry and I discussed how to combine literacy skills with his unit on chemistry. He wanted me to give the pretest before Spring Break because he planned to initiate the chemistry unit and teach it during the month of April. He encouraged me to be certain the pretest was fun but challenging and offered to help me develop it.*

**March 17**  *"Literacy Partners" is a state guide for library media programs. It contains a list of information skill objectives by grade level. When I reviewed the middle school objectives, there were several that seemed relevant to activities he had planned for the chemistry unit. Citing sources of information used in projects and papers is a concern with grades six through eight. Other related eighth grade objectives were*

- *Identify award winning products and people.*
- *Employ Boolean operators in conducting an online search.*
- *Summarize information from several sources and document each source.*

*After showing Mr. Berry the information literacy objectives I had identified, he seemed excited and offered to help me prepare the pretest. We worked on it for two periods. I typed the test and he made an answer key. We scheduled the pretest for March 21st.*

**March 21**  *Mr. Berry brought his class into the media center and explained that we were going to combine chemistry with literacy skills development. He explained they were going to take a pretest. I distributed pencils while he passed out the tests and answer cards. The test took approximately 20 minutes. When the students had finished taking the test, Mr. Berry went to the classroom to scan the answer sheets while I explained the correct answers. When he returned with the results, the students were shocked by their poor performance. I assured them this score was a pretest and after Spring Break they would visit the library and improve their skills. I was shocked at the 60 percent and 64.7 percent that the two classes scored on their Scantron literacy skills/chemistry pretest.*

**March 30**  *Mr. Berry began the chemistry unit today with a preview of the textbook chapter. Afterwards, he assigned an element for each student to research, explaining they were to report what they learned to the class. For this assignment, they were to use library books and the Internet. To get them started, he provided a list of Internet sites to use that included*

- <http://www.schoolnotes.com/35243/berry/html>
- <www.chemsoc.org/viselements/>
- <www.chemlab.pc.maricopa.edu/periodic/periodic.html>
- <www.periodic.lanl.gov/listl.html>

**April 1-4**  *Mr. Berry's students began their search for information on their assigned element. When a student came to the library, we discussed the type of information needed, where the information might be found, and what she might learn about the element.*

**April 8-9**  *Classes were suspended because students were taking the state-mandated Stanford Achievement Test. This year they are taking a new version, #10. I was busy monitoring a group of test-takers in the library.*
*When I reported to Mr. Berry that only half of his class had used the library for research, he decided to schedule a class visit on April 11th.*

**April 11**  *When Mr. Berry's class came to the library, I demonstrated a Boolean search for specific elements using Yahoo and Google. I followed with a demonstration search of Access Science, which is part of the state's online library. After the search demonstrations, I showed the students how to read, interpret, and connect the information without plagiarizing. We discussed the use of quotes and how to credit quoted information.*

**April 22**  *Mr. Berry told me he reminded the students to correctly cite the information they used for their papers about the elements.*

**April 23**  *I told Mr. Berry that the information skills his students had developed while studying chemistry were now being applied in a history project. His students were using Boolean searches to locate information for their social studies fair projects.*

**April 28** *Mr. Berry and I decided to do a quick skills check. Each student was given a research assignment to be completed in five minutes or less. It would be a pass/fail grade. The assignment required each student to*

- *Find a Pulitzer Prize winner in chemistry.*
- *Find a quote by that chemist.*
- *Cite works by that chemist.*

*Despite the time limit, all students were required to complete the tasks. Those who completed it within the allotted time received a passing grade but all the students had a feeling of accomplishment when they completed the tasks.*

**May 5** *Mr. Berry gave students in his 7th and 8th period classes a posttest covering chemistry and information skills. After the sheets were scanned, he reported the 7th period average was 83 percent and the 8th period average was 80 percent. (See the pretest and posttest on the pages that follow.)*

## Testing Measures

### Pretest for Information Skills on Chemistry

Do not write on your test, but color in the correct answer on your Scantron card. Use a number 2 pencil. Write your name, your code name, date, test number and period on your answer card. Select the best answer for each item and return the test to Mrs. Churchill when finished.

1) Where would one locate the 1995 winner of the Nobel Prize for Chemistry?
   a. Encyclopedia
   b. Almanac
   c. Card catalog
   d. Eighth grade science textbook

2) Paul Crutzen, Mario Molina, and F. Sherwood Rowland, the winners of the Nobel Prize for Chemistry, won with their atmospheric chemistry, particularly concerning the formation and decomposition of ozone. To locate information on their work, one would search the Internet with the following Boolean search:
   a. Paul Crutzen OR Mario Molina OR F. Sherwood Rowland
   b. Paul Crutzen AND Mario Molina AND F. Sherwood Rowland AND Nobel Prize
   c. Nobel Prize OR ozone
   d. Nobel Prize OR ozone OR atmospheric chemistry

3) Pesticide manufactures must comply with certain safety standards. If pesticide gasses were escaping into the environment, what government agency would one write?
   a. The U.S. Fish and Wildlife Services
   b. The Department of the Interior
   c. The Environmental Protection Agency
   d. The Food and Drug Administration

4) If current U.S. policies and laws on chemical or biological weapons were needed for a class discussion, where would one search?
   a. Infoplease.com
   b. Congressional Record
   c. CNN.com
   d. National Archive and Records Administration

5) Where would one locate David McCord's famous lines spoken in 1935, "The cricket's gone, we only hear machines; In erg and atom they exact their pay. And life is largely lived on silver screens, and chemistry anneals the common clay."
   a. Ebscoweb Host
   b. Almanac

    c.   Bartlett's Familiar Quotations

    d.   Encyclopedia

6) If one needed chemical compound information on table salt, his Boolean search would include:
    a.   Chemistry and salt
    b.   Salt
    c.   Salt but not table salt
    d.   NaCl and table salt

7) If Nitrates are found near Machu Picchu, Peru, in South America, but one doesn't know where that city is, he or she is to use:
    a.   Glossary, alphabetical order, and page number to locate the city
    b.   An atlas, table of contents, map, index, and page to locate the city
    c.   An almanac, index, and page number to locate the city
    d.   An atlas, table of contents, map, index of the map, and gridlines to locate the city

8) What type of graph is illustrated below?
    a.   Line graph
    b.   Circle graph
    c.   Bar graph
    d.   Pictograph

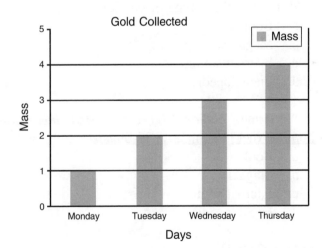

9) In the above illustration, a certain amount of gold was collected. What is the mean?
    a.   1.0
    b.   2.0
    c.   2.5
    d.   3.0

10) Which group of elements combines to fluorine best?
   a. Noble gases
   b. Other halogens
   c. Alkaline metals
   d. All of the above

11) This citation example: Knapp, Brian. *Silicon*. Danbury, Connecticut: Grolier, 1996.
   a. Is a book
   b. Is a magazine
   c. Is an Internet source
   d. Is an encyclopedia

12) The quote, "Seawater contains more than 70 elements dissolved in mineral form." comes from *Popular Science*. This is what type of resource? "Water: The Universal Solvent." *The New Book of Popular Science*. Danbury, Connecticut: Grolier, 2000.
   a. Book
   b. Magazine
   c. Internet source
   d. Encyclopedia

13) Fortner, Bryan. "Water Vapor Almost Busts Dam." *Popular Science*. March 2003: 94. What type of citation is this?
   a. Book
   b. Magazine
   c. Internet source
   d. Encyclopedia

14) "Fluorine." *National Library of Medicine*. 8 May 2002. Toxnet. 19 Mar. 2003, <hppt://toxnet.nlm.nih.gov/cgi-bin/sis/search> is a
   a. Book
   b. Magazine
   c. Internet source
   d. Encyclopedia

15) $H_2 + O_2 \rightarrow H_2O$
   a. Balanced
   b. Combustible
   c. Covalent
   d. None of the above

## Posttest for Information Skills on Chemistry

Do not write on your test, but color in the correct answer on your Scantron card. Use a number 2 pencil for this Scantron test. Write your name, your code name, date, test number, and period on your answer card. Select the best answer and return the test to Mrs. Churchill.

1) Where would one locate the 2001 winner of the Nobel Prize for Chemistry?
   a. Encyclopedia
   b. Almanac
   c. Card catalog
   d. Eighth grade science textbook

2) Marie Curie won the Nobel Prize for her discovery of radium and its uses in nature. To locate information on Marie Curie and her work on this award-winning discovery, one would search the Internet with the following Boolean search:
   a. Marie Curie
   b. Marie Curie AND Nobel Prize AND radium
   c. Nobel Prize OR radium
   d. Nobel Prize AND chemistry

3) Styrofoam manufacturers must comply with certain safety standards. If Chlorofluorocarbons were escaping into the environment, what government agency would one write to?
   a. The U.S. Fish and Wildlife Services
   b. The Department of the Interior
   c. The Environmental Protection Agency
   d. The Food and Drug Administration

4) Where would one go to find current biochemical research on SARS?
   a. Infoplease.com
   b. CDC.gov
   c. CNN.com
   d. National Archives and Records Administration

5) What type of graph is illustrated here?
   a. Bar graph
   b. Line graph
   c. Circle graph
   d. Pie chart

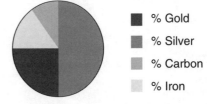

6) Which element is the most commonly collected from the above graph?
   a. Gold
   b. Silver
   c. Carbon
   d. Iron

7) The following citation example: Knapp, Brian. *Oxygen*. Danbury, Connecticut: Grolier, 2000 is a
   a. Book
   b. Magazine
   c. Internet source
   d. Encyclopedia

8) The quote, "By far the worst accident in nuclear-reactor history occurred on April 26, 1986, when a reactor in the Chernobyl complex near Kiev, Ukraine, exploded and caught fire," comes from "Nuclear Energy: Nuclear Accidents." *The New Book of Popular Science*. Danbury, Connecticut: Grolier, 2000. This is what type of resource?
   a. Book
   b. Magazine
   c. Internet source
   d. Encyclopedia

9) The current quote, "Then there are the malodrants, the chemical brews that mimic revolting smells and can disperse attackers and crowds." Comes from Adams, Eric. "Shoot to not kill." *Popular Science,* May 2003: 89-93.
   a. Book
   b. Magazine
   c. Internet source
   d. Encyclopedia

10) "Chlorine." National Library of Medicine. 8 May 2002. Toxnet. 19 Mar. 2003. <http://toxnet.nlm.nih.gov/cgi-bin/sis/search>.
   a. Book
   b. Magazine
   c. Internet source
   d. Encyclopedia

# Experience #2

## Berry Middle School, Hoover City Schools, Alabama

### Description of School and Students

Berry Middle School is one of three middle schools within the rapidly growing and changing Hoover City School system in Alabama, a satellite city just south of Birmingham. The school facility is a remodeled high school building that easily accommodates the 1,000 students who attend. Berry's diverse student body comes from all over the United States and the world. The students are mostly high performers. They continually score well on state-mandated achievement measures such as the Stanford Achievement Test and the Alabama Direct Assessment of Writing. Seeing the work of individual students in literary magazines and similar publications gives evidence and is an important carryover from the impressive writing assessment scores.

### Description of Cooperating Teacher

Miss Rachel LaMonte is a former elementary teacher who moved to Berry Middle School four years ago. She teaches sixth graders the language arts curriculum as mandated by the Alabama State Department of Education and put forth in its curriculum guide. This year the school faculty and administration elected to move to a new instructional model, "Reading in the Content Area" program. The change was made because students were not performing as well as they should on the standardized reading test. Most middle schools do not teach reading as a separate course like it is taught in elementary schools. The faculty believed sixth grade students needed reading instruction, particularly in textual reading, so they designed and implemented the new program. All sixth grade teachers would continue teaching their discipline, but they would also teach reading strategies within the context of their discipline. The sixth grade was divided into four sections. Each grading period a section rotates to a different discipline so that through the year, all students were taught math, science, social studies, and language arts as well as having reading instruction in each of those content areas. During the year, Miss LaMonte taught Reading in Language Arts to approximately 100 students. The model appears to be successful and administrators from other schools in the area have visited the school to see the program in action.

### Library Media Services

The library media center is the heart of the building and instructional program at Berry. It serves as the center for reading, research, and technology integration. On a typical day, students come to the library before the school day begins to get help choosing new reading or research books, or to complete a technology project, or to locate articles and pictures on the Alabama Virtual Library databases or the Internet, or to print work completed at home the night before. The day for many students begins in the media center. The mornings before school begins mirror the type of activities that occur throughout the day.

The media specialist appreciates how the media program has grown out of the instructional needs of the students and teachers. A good example of how a school emphasis influences media center priorities is the current school focus on reading in the content areas. This priority has required purchase of materials to support that change. Ironically, stressing reading in the content areas has resulted in all students reading more fiction. An ever-present challenge is the insatiable thirst for new titles that cover a wide range of reading levels. For four years, the Berry students have met their reading goals, and earned a school-wide trip to a historical theatre in Birmingham to see a current movie.

As funds allow, the library media specialist works with the Library Committee to invite authors to visit the school and share their work with students. Students especially enjoy getting the authors to autograph a book. Authors are selected whose works appeal to all grades at the school. A packet of suggested activities is developed and given to each teacher well before the author's visit. The packet suggests projects for students to do that are related to the author's work.

## The Collaborative Project

Early in the year, Miss LaMonte and I talked briefly about how teaching information literacy skills could be incorporated into Reading in the Language Arts. Having transferred from an elementary school where students had a rigidly-scheduled library period with activities unrelated to classroom concerns, she had not collaborated with a media specialist. During our initial conversation about the new course, Miss LaMonte confided that she was concerned because research was one part of her instructional responsibility according to the Alabama Course of Study for sixth grade. It was music to my ears when she said, "You're going to have to help me; I've never incorporated database searches and bibliographies before." Naturally, I readily agreed and we scheduled a time to meet.

During our first planning session, we decided that research fit perfectly with the Reading in the Language Arts Content class. It would give students good practice in skimming, scanning, and selecting main ideas. Since writing in the content is part of the reading strategies class, they would be able to practice that also. Our joint project would be to have the students undertake a research project. Miss LaMonte wanted the topic for each student to be of individual interest, although within certain constraints. Her approach to teaching is to individualize instruction whenever possible. She also wanted each student's topic to center on a social issue, unless a student had a very good reason to choose something different. From the media center perspective, I suggested the students might need some guidance in order to alleviate any frustrations caused by not being able to locate adequate materials in the library to support age-appropriate, social issues topics. We decided that a list of suggested topics would be a good starting place.

In keeping with the developmental level of her sixth graders, Miss LaMonte wanted to stay away from a formal written paper and she liked my idea of incorporating technology into the presentations. After reviewing the options, we decided the students should create a public service brochure. Since she is very skilled in technology, she decided that this would make the process more engaging and interesting for her students. This project would also fulfill one of the requirements of the Alabama technology curriculum. Students were provided a blank brochure as a model so they would understand the amount of space available for their content. Each student would select a social issue as a topic. Each brochure would have a definition of the problem on one panel, what causes the problem and why on a second panel, who it affects on the third panel, and possible solutions on the fourth panel. We needed a list of suggested topics for students to consider.

So it was back to the library media center for me. I knew right away that most of the books would be in the 300 section of the Dewey Classification System. When the list of topics was ready, I informed Miss LaMonte and asked if I could give a short pretest to determine her students' level of information literacy. The pretest would be written especially for this class. The objectives of the test were to determine the students' skills in using the electronic catalog, the dictionary, and magazine databases. Items included on the test would also determine student knowledge about note-taking and citing sources for a bibliography. *Literacy Partners*, a book published by the state education agency, sets information skill objectives for each grade. According to this document, the sixth graders should have learned the following objectives when they were in the fifth grade:

- Use guidewords, keys, and search terms to retrieve information efficiently.
- Use cross-references to locate additional information.
- Retrieve information about a given topic from sources in different formats.
- Write paragraphs and stories to dramatize a point, experience, or opinion.

The pretest would let Miss LaMonte and I know if we needed to provide some remedial instruction. So the test was drafted, reviewed by us, and prepared for distribution in the classroom. Our principal also wanted parents to be informed that I would be writing about the project and to get their approval to proceed. These letters were also distributed to students as they returned their tests. The letters were returned in a timely manner. Although parental involvement is unusual in a collaborative venture, and only occurred this time because the information would be published, it proved to be a motivating force.

## Project Diary

**March 31** *Miss LaMonte accompanied her class to the library. She explained the research project, distributed the list of suggested topics, and a rubric that would be used to evaluate each student's final project. I administered an information literacy pretest. Later that day I scored the pretest and found that students were familiar with the concepts of searching for information by author, subject, and title. They knew how to locate books using those entry points in Athena, the library's database, but they were not adequately knowledgeable in locating information in magazines, note taking, or documenting sources. This told us what we would need to emphasize as we went through the research process. In addition, the information skills curriculum guide for the sixth grade specifies the following objectives:*

- *Use a style manual to determine appropriate punctuation and capitalization.*
- *Use current event sources to retrieve and substantiate facts and statistics.*
- *Use online information tools for research and problem solving.*
- *Evaluate the accuracy and comprehensiveness of various information sources.*
- *Identify the parts of a citation in a bibliography or list of cited works.*

*So it seemed the project's objectives were in line with the mandated curriculum and with students needs. Later in the day, Miss LaMonte came to the library to schedule class visits to the library to browse and select topics. I liked the fact that students would be given plenty of time for pre-searching and deciding on a topic. This is an important step that is often overlooked and Kuhlthau's work has underscored its importance.*

**April 7-9** *Using the suggested list of topics, students began locating and scanning books to decide what interested them. One student is an artist and expressed a desire to do her research on a famous artist. Even though this topic did not involve a social issue, it did fit with the teacher's desire to allow students to follow individual interests, so her topic was approved. All students were able to decide on their topics within the three-day schedule for topic selection.*

**April 22** *Using EBSCO Middle Search, which is available online in our school through the state-supported Alabama Virtual Library, I began instructing students in conducting a database search. An entire class period was spent on locating, evaluating, and printing at least one article. The teacher and I had decided to limit students to Middle Search because the articles are age appropriate for sixth graders. Students had to skim and scan to decide which articles were the best to print. This activity was good reinforcement in those reading strategies.*

**April 23** *The following day I introduced SIRS Knowledge Source, a second electronic database. Students, especially those with social issue topics, learned what a valuable resource this database was.*

**April 24** *Today we spent time learning how to evaluate useful Internet sites. This was a tough one! We quickly found that students thought anything on the Internet was fine. Because of time constraints, the development level of sixth graders, and their topics we discovered that it worked to restrict them by the domains, ".edu," ".org," and ".gov."*

*By this date, every student had at least one book, one magazine article from Middle Search, one item from SIRS Knowledge Source, and at least one Internet source. Using the resources they had found, they were ready to go to the classroom and read for main ideas. Since this is a reading class, Miss LaMonte wanted them to spend most of their time on the reading aspect of the project. They were required to write down facts from the library resources and to highlight important information in the printouts.*

**April 27** *Miss LaMonte shared the students' work with me and it was fascinating to see how much better this class was in using reading strategies than earlier groups had been. I remembered that this class had already had reading in mathematics, science, and social studies before starting Miss LaMonte's Reading in Language Arts Content. The biggest difference was in the amount of information highlighted as the main ideas. Earlier classes pretty much highlighted everything. In fact, an entire page might be highlighted in yellow. But this class had highlighted much less on each article, indicating they were able to pick out the most important information using less and less words.*

*In the note taking process, some students had trouble distinguishing between information they found and their personal opinion. This reaction was especially true on some topics. The topic, school uniforms, is a good example. Students who chose that topic were very passionate about it. "Why can't I say what I think?" they would often ask. They maintained that students needed to be asked their opinions; after all, they are the ones wearing the uniforms. It took some work on everyone's part, but the students were eventually able to keep fact and opinion separate in their brochures.*

**April 28** *A few of the students found their articles were not helpful and returned individually to go online to locate better sources. It was rewarding to see them come in by themselves and do this with no help from anyone.*

**May 3-5** *Miss LaMonte and I had decided that we would team teach how to write a citation and how to make a bibliography, with me facilitating the lessons. For three days she brought the class to the library's classroom and students worked using the actual sources they had used in getting information for their projects. Students used the resources to write the data for each resource onto a note card.*

**May 6** *The students entered their bibliographic information directly onto the resources panel of their brochure. This approach worked wonderfully with less frustration on the part of the students than having them enter the information at home. We decided that that is the way to do it in the future.*

**May 8** *In the classroom, students were asked to complete a self-evaluation form with questions composed by the teacher and the library media specialist. I was interested in knowing if there was a difference between pretest performance and what they knew after completing their projects. To my delight, students showed improvement in understanding how to document a source and how to locate current information in magazines using the Alabama Virtual Library.*

**May 10** *Looking back on the experience, I realize the teacher and I worked together throughout the research process with each of us facilitating it at different points along the way. The teacher was very pleased with how well the process had worked and also with the end result (brochure). I am delighted about the opportunity to work with the students on their information literacy skills, and I believe they made progress that will enrich their studies as they continue through school.*

## Project Evaluation

Each student's project was evaluated by Miss LaMonte using a rubric. In addition, each student was asked to complete a self-evaluation form to help Miss LaMonte and me determine how they felt about the project and their performance.

Table 9.1

## Self Evaluation for Research Brochure Project

Name: _____ Date: _____

_____

Topic: _____

_____

**Please respond honestly, thoroughly, and in complete sentences to the following questions. The only unacceptable answers are: "I don't know," "Nothing," and other similar answers. This form will be graded and the grade will be based on whether you followed the directions.**

What did you learn that you did not already know about locating, evaluating, and using information? Please be specific about what you learned. There is no one who knows everything about the researching process (including Mrs. Mason). _____

_____

_____

_____

Explain how you were challenged while doing this assignment. In other words, what was the most difficult part of the project? Please be fairly specific and do not respond, "typing." _____

_____

_____

_____

Did you complete the daily assignments to the best of your ability? Why or why not? _____

_____

_____

_____

Do you believe you used your time wisely in the classroom and the computer lab? Why or why not? _____

_____

_____

_____

Table 9.1

## Self Evaluation for Research Brochure Project continued

Did you feel like you had enough time in class to complete the daily assignments? If not, what could be done to make things more manageable?

_____

_____

_____

What might you change about this assignment? If you say, "nothing," then what parts of the assignment do you think are the most important?

_____

_____

_____

How would you rate yourself on this assignment, grade-wise? Explain why you would give yourself this grade. _____

_____

_____

_____

Look at your reading strategies handout on page 1 of your reading binder. Pick out AT LEAST three of the reading strategies that you used and explain how each helped you during the research process.

     Strategy #1: _____

     How it helped you: _____

     _____

     Strategy #2: _____

     How it helped you: _____

     _____

     Strategy #3: _____

     How it helped you: _____

     _____

What suggestions or information might you give a peer who is about to start this project? _____

_____

_____

# Looking Back

One year following the experiences described in this chapter, Lisa and Lucy were asked to revisit the experiences and to explain what happened in year two. Their responses remind us that constant change is part of an educator's life. Unlike factory work where change is occasional, change in schools is continuous, which means educators must learn to adapt.

### Lisa Churchill

Acclimating a new colleague to a collaborative project was refreshing and worthwhile because Mr. Berry and his students were successful. Evidence of their success was most apparent by his desire to repeat the experience and their test scores. However, I learned never to be content about collaborative planning because things change and people move. Last year, I felt as though "all my ducks were in a row" because all the faculty members were planning collaboratively with me to some degree. Then things, beyond my control, began to change. Vestavia City annexed housing areas formerly in Jefferson County. As a result, 150 students who attended our school were transferred to a Vestavia City school. Seven teachers elected to move from our school to the Vestavia City school the Gresham students would attend. Next, our principal was transferred to a high school position in the county system and four teachers followed him, including Mr. Berry who was offered a position teaching biology and chemistry. Our school lost 11 teachers but hired seven new ones. For me, this meant a loss of 11 teachers who were oriented to collaborative planning and the challenge of recruiting seven new teachers. It was a bittersweet reminder that the task of collaborative planning never ends. To date, I have a first-year English teacher and a social studies teacher who are interested in collaborating on projects where students will learn information skills as they learn course content. This means I only have five teachers who are not collaborating.

### Lucy Mason

Planning is definitely ongoing, even this year. Miss LaMonte and I are always changing what we do in different parts of this project. We have evidence that the school administration definitely supports and encourages collaborative planning. The library schedule is totally flexible and teachers have opportunities to plan with me during the regular school day. We are not so concrete on the lesson plan being written in stone because we change things all of the time. Miss LaMonte and I both monitored student progress and worked with them through the unit. My role in assessment involved checking work as they worked in the lab and making suggestions for improvement before the project was complete. This year, I had an ESL (English as a Second Language) student who came after school for some individual work to help him understand the material. Group management is, of course, a team process. The teacher and I just talk about or e-mail each other any concerns we have, and revise our plans as change is needed. Throughout the two years we have been doing this project, the library has updated its resources on the topics used. The students not only learn to locate all of the resources related to their topic; they also learn to evaluate them for accurateness and usefulness. The main skills they develop or refine during this project are skimming, scanning, highlighting, and extracting main ideas for their brochures. By the time their brochures are finished, students have not only engaged in higher order thinking, but they also have learned to retrieve information from the library database, from many of the Alabama Virtual Library databases, and from the Internet. As Miss LaMonte and I review the products and use the rubric to judge them, we look forward to the next semester. However, this year we will collaborate on the brochure project for the last time because I will retire at the end of this school year. It makes me sad to think about this change because I enjoy working with teachers like Miss LaMonte.